DOVER · THRIFT · EDITIONS

The Long Voyage Home and Other Plays

EUGENE O'NEILL

DOVER PUBLICATIONS, INC.
New York

DOVER THRIFT EDITIONS

GENERAL EDITOR: STANLEY APPELBAUM
EDITOR OF THIS VOLUME: ALAN WEISSMAN

Copyright

Theatrical Rights

Bibliographical Note

This Dover edition, first published in 1995, is an unabridged republication of *The Moon of the Caribbees, Bound East for Cardiff, The Long Voyage Home* and *In the Zone*, all originally published by Boni & Liveright, New York, in the volume *The Moon of the Caribbees and Six Other Plays of the Sea*, 1919. A new Note has been written specially for this edition.

Library of Congress Cataloging-in-Publication Data

O'Neill, Eugene, 1888–1953.
   [Plays. Selections]
   The long voyage home and other plays / Eugene O'Neill.
      p.   cm. — (Dover thrift editions)
   Originally published: New York : Boni & Liveright, 1919.
   Contents: The moon of the Caribbees — Bound east for Cardiff — The long voyage home — In the zone.
   ISBN 0-486-28755-6 (pbk.)
   I. Title. II. Series.
PS3529.N5A6 1995b
812'.52—dc20
                                         95-35219
                                           CIP

Manufactured in the United States of America
Dover Publications, Inc., 31 East 2nd Street, Mineola, N.Y. 11501

Note

It is often said that nothing of literary value written by an American for the American stage was performed there before the plays of Eugene O'Neill came along. This assertion, if not literally true, is very nearly so, for the vast majority of the plays written by Americans and publicly performed in this country before and for two decades after the turn of the century were sentimental melodramas, low-grade farces or other vehicles of light entertainment.

Beyond the Horizon (1920) was the first of O'Neill's many plays to be performed on Broadway. The actual beginning of his public career was, however, experienced only by the fortunate few who saw a performance of *Bound East for Cardiff* by the Provincetown Players in Provincetown, Massachusetts, in February 1916, or a few months later in New York. In the next few years this influential group performed a number of O'Neill's one-act plays, to the benefit of both O'Neill's reputation and their own. Four of these plays (including *Bound East for Cardiff*) are reprinted here. These little dramas, O'Neill's first important works, are linked by a number of characters that appear in more than one and to that degree make the plays a series. All of these characters work on the S.S. *Glencairn*, a British tramp steamer, aboard which the action of three of the four plays is set.

Each of these dramas tells a different story and evokes a different mood but all are marked by economy of structure, careful attention to dialogue, and a gritty naturalism hitherto unknown — except for a few foreign imports — on the American stage.

The four plays were written between 1913 and 1917 and first published in 1919 (in 1924 they were published under the collective title S.S. *Glencairn*). The order in which they appear here is that in which the incidents enacted are supposed to have occurred.

Contents

The Moon of the Caribbees

A PLAY IN ONE ACT

CHARACTERS

YANK
DRISCOLL
OLSON
DAVIS } *Seamen of the British tramp steamer,*
COCKY *Glencairn.*
SMITTY
PAUL

LAMPS, *the lamptrimmer.*
CHIPS, *the carpenter.*
OLD TOM, *the donkeyman.*

BIG FRANK
DICK } *Firemen on the* Glencairn.
MAX
PADDY

BELLA
SUSIE } *West Indian Negresses.*
VIOLET
PEARL

THE FIRST MATE

Two other seamen — SCOTTY AND IVAN — and several
other members of the stokehole-engine-room crew.

NOTE. — With the exception of "In the Zone," the action of all the plays in this volume takes place in years preceding the outbreak of the World War.

SCENE — A *forward section of the main deck of the British tramp steamer*
Glencairn, *at anchor off an island in the West Indies. The full moon,
half-way up the sky, throws a clear light on the deck. The sea is calm
and the ship motionless.*

*On the left two of the derrick booms of the foremast jut out at an
angle of forty-five degrees, black against the sky. In the rear the dark
outline of the port bulwark is sharply defined against a distant strip
of coral beach, white in the moonlight, fringed with coco palms
whose tops rise clear of the horizon. On the right is the forecastle with
an open doorway in the center leading to the seamen's and firemen's
compartments. On either side of the doorway are two closed doors
opening on the quarters of the Bo'sun, the ship's carpenter, the
messroom steward, and the donkeyman — what might be called the
petty officers of the ship. Near each bulwark there is also a short
stairway, like a section of fire escape, leading up to the forecastle
head (the top of the forecastle) — the edge of which can be seen on
the right.*

*In the center of the deck, and occupying most of the space, is the
large, raised square of the number one hatch, covered with canvas,
battened down for the night.*

*A melancholy negro chant, faint and far-off, drifts, crooning, over
the water.*

*Most of the seamen and firemen are reclining or sitting on the
hatch.* PAUL *is leaning against the port bulwark, the upper part of his
stocky figure outlined against the sky.* SMITTY *and* COCKY *are sitting*

3

on the edge of the forecastle head with their legs dangling over. Nearly all are smoking pipes or cigarettes. The majority are dressed in patched suits of dungaree. Quite a few are in their bare feet and some of them, especially the firemen, have nothing on but a pair of pants and an undershirt. A good many wear caps.

There is the low murmur of different conversations going on in the separate groups as the curtain rises. This is followed by a sudden silence in which the singing from the land can be plainly heard.

DRISCOLL — [*A powerfully built Irishman who is sitting on the edge of the hatch, front — irritably.*] Will ye listen to them naygurs? I wonder now, do they call that keenin' a song?

SMITTY — [*A young Englishman with a blond mustache. He is sitting on the forecastle head looking out over the water with his chin supported on his hands.*] It doesn't make a chap feel very cheerful, does it? [*He sighs.*]

COCKY — [*A wizened runt of a man with a straggling gray mustache — slapping* SMITTY *on the back.*] Cheero, ole dear! Down't be ser dawn in the marf, Duke. She loves yer.

SMITTY — [*Gloomily.*] Shut up, Cocky! [*He turns away from* COCKY *and falls to dreaming again, staring toward the spot on shore where the singing seems to come from.*]

BIG FRANK — [*A huge fireman sprawled out on the right of the hatch — waving a hand toward the land.*] They bury somebody — py chiminy Christmas, I tink so from way it sound.

YANK — [*A rather good-looking rough who is sitting beside* DRISCOLL.] What d'yuh mean, bury? They don't plant 'em down here, Dutchy. They eat 'em to save fun'ral expenses. I guess this guy went down the wrong way an' they got indigestion.

COCKY — Indigestion! Ho yus, not 'arf! Down't yer know as them blokes 'as two stomacks like a bleedin' camel?

DAVIS — [*A short, dark man seated on the right of hatch.*] An' you seen the two, I s'pect, ain't you?

COCKY — [*Scornfully.*] Down't be showin' yer igerance be tryin' to make a mock o' me what has seen more o' the world than yeself ever will.

MAX — [*A Swedish fireman — from the rear of hatch.*] Spin dat yarn, Cocky.

COCKY — It's Gawd's troof, what I tole yer. I 'eard it from a bloke what was captured pris'ner by 'em in the Solomon Islands. Shipped wiv 'im one voyage. 'Twas a rare treat to 'ear 'im tell what 'appened to 'im among 'em. [*Musingly.*] 'E was a funny bird, 'e was — 'ailed from Mile End, 'e did.

DRISCOLL — [*With a snort.*] Another lyin' Cockney, the loike av yourself!

LAMPS — [*A fat Swede who is sitting on a camp stool in front of his door talking with* CHIPS.] Where you meet up with him, Cocky?

CHIPS — [*A lanky Scotchman — derisively.*] In New Guinea, I'll lay my oath!

COCKY — [*Defiantly.*] Yus! It *was* in New Guinea, time I was ship-wrecked there. [*There is a perfect storm of groans and laughter at this speech.*]

YANK — [*Getting up.*] Yuh know what we said yuh'd get if yuh sprung any of that lyin' New Guinea dope on us again, don't yuh? Close that trap if yuh don't want a duckin' over the side.

COCKY — Ow, I was on'y tryin' to edicate yer a bit. [*He sinks into dignified silence.*]

YANK — [*Nodding toward the shore.*] Don't yuh know this is the West Indies, yuh crazy mut? There ain't no cannibals here. They're only common niggers.

DRISCOLL — [*Irritably.*] Whativir they are, the divil take their cryin'. It's enough to give a man the jigs listenin' to 'em.

YANK — [*With a grin.*] What's the matter, Drisc? Yuh're as sore as a boil about somethin'.

DRISCOLL — I'm dyin' wid impatience to have a dhrink; an' that blarsted bumboat naygur woman took her oath she'd bring back rum enough for the lot av us whin she came back on board to-night.

BIG FRANK — [*Overhearing this — in a loud eager voice.*] You say the bumboat voman vill bring booze?

DRISCOLL — [*Sarcastically.*] That's right — tell the Old Man about ut, an' the Mate, too. [*All of the crew have edged nearer to* DRISCOLL *and are listening to the conversation with an air of suppressed excitement.* DRISCOLL *lowers his voice impressively and addresses them all.*] She said she cud snake ut on board in the bottoms av thim baskets av fruit they're goin' to bring wid 'em to sell to us for'ard.

THE DONKEYMAN — [*An old gray-headed man with a kindly, wrinkled face. He is sitting on a camp stool in front of his door, right front.*] She'll be bringin' some black women with her this time—or times has changed since I put in here last.

DRISCOLL—She said she wud—two or three—more, maybe, I dunno. [*This announcement is received with great enthusiasm by all hands.*]

COCKY—Wot a bloody lark!

OLSON—Py yingo, we have one hell of a time!

DRISCOLL—[*Warningly.*] Remimber ye must be quiet about ut, ye scuts—wid the dhrink, I mane—ivin if the bo'sun is ashore. The Old Man ordered her to bring no booze on board or he wudn't buy a thing off av her for the ship.

PADDY—[*A squat, ugly Liverpool Irishman.*] To the divil wid him!

BIG FRANK—[*Turning on him.*] Shud up, you tamn fool, Paddy! You vant make trouble? [*To* DRISCOLL.] You und me, ve keep dem quiet, Drisc.

DRISCOLL—Right ye are, Dutchy. I'll split the skull av the first wan av ye starts to foight. [*Three bells are heard striking.*]

DAVIS—Three bells. When's she comin', Drisc?

DRISCOLL—She'll be here any minute now, surely. [*To* PAUL, *who has returned to his position by the bulwark after hearing* DRISCOLL'S *news.*] D'you see 'em comin', Paul?

PAUL—I don't see anyting like bumboat. [*They all set themselves to wait, lighting pipes, cigarettes, and making themselves comfortable. There is a silence broken only by the mournful singing of the negroes on shore.*]

SMITTY—[*Slowly—with a trace of melancholy.*] I wish they'd stop that song. It makes you think of—well—things you ought to forget. Rummy go, what?

COCKY—[*Slapping him on the back.*] Cheero, ole love! We'll be 'avin our rum in arf a mo', Duke. [*He comes down to the deck, leaving* SMITTY *alone on the forecastle head.*]

BIG FRANK—Sing someting, Drisc. Den ve don't hear dot yelling.

DAVIS—Give us a chanty, Drisc.

PADDY—Wan all av us knows.

MAX—We all sing in on chorus.

OLSON—"Rio Grande," Drisc.

BIG FRANK—No, ve don't know dot. Sing "Viskey Johnny."

CHIPS — "Flyin' Cloud."

COCKY — Now! Guv us "Maid o' Amsterdam."

LAMPS — "Santa Anna" iss good one.

DRISCOLL — Shut your mouths, all av you. [*Scornfully.*] A chanty is ut ye want? I'll bet me whole pay day there's not wan in the crowd 'ceptin' Yank here, an' Ollie, an' meself, an' Lamps an' Cocky, maybe, wud be sailors enough to know the main from the mizzen on a windjammer. Ye've heard the names av chanties but divil a note av the tune or a loine av the words do ye know. There's hardly a rale deep-water sailor lift on the seas, more's the pity.

YANK — Give us "Blow The Man Down." We all know some of that. [*A chorus of assenting voices:* Yes! — Righto! — Let 'er drive! Start 'er, Drisc! *etc.*]

DRISCOLL — Come in then, all av ye. [*He sings:*]
As I was a-roamin' down Paradise Street —

ALL — Wa-a-ay, blow the man down!

DRISCOLL — As I was a-roamin' down Paradise Street —

ALL — Give us some time to blow the man down!

CHORUS

Blow the man down, boys, oh, blow the man down!
Wa-a-ay, blow the man down!
As I was a-roamin' down Paradise Street —
Give us some time to blow the man down!

DRISCOLL — A pretty young maiden I chanced for to meet.

ALL — Wa-a-ay, blow the man down!

DRISCOLL — A pretty young maiden I chanced for to meet.

ALL — Give us some time to blow the man down!

CHORUS

Blow the man down, boys, oh, blow the man down!
Wa-a-ay, blow the man down!
A pretty young maiden I chanced for to meet.
Give us some time to blow the man down!

PAUL — [*Just as Driscoll is clearing his throat preparatory to starting the next verse.*] Hay, Drisc! Here she come, I tink. Some bumboat comin' dis way. [*They all rush to the side and look toward the land.*]

YANK — There's five or six of them in it — and they paddle like skirts.

DRISCOLL — [*Wildly elated.*] Hurroo, ye scuts! 'Tis thim right enough. [*He does a few jig steps on the deck.*]

OLSON — [*After a pause during which all are watching the approaching boat.*] Py yingo, I see six in boat, yes, sir.

DAVIS — I kin make out the baskets. See 'em there amidships?

BIG FRANK — Vot kind booze dey bring — viskey?

DRISCOLL — Rum, foine West Indy rum wid a kick in ut loike a mule's hoind leg.

LAMPS — Maybe she don't bring any; maybe skipper scare her.

DRISCOLL — Don't be throwin' cold water, Lamps. I'll skin her black hoide off av her if she goes back on her worrd.

YANK — Here they come. Listen to 'em gigglin'. [*Calling.*] Oh, you kiddo! [*The sound of women's voices can be heard talking and laughing.*]

DRISCOLL — [*Calling.*] Is ut you, Mrs. Old Black Joe?

A WOMAN'S VOICE — Ullo, Mike! [*There is loud feminine laughter at this retort.*]

DRISCOLL — Shake a leg an' come abord thin.

THE WOMAN'S VOICE — We're a-comin'.

DRISCOLL — Come on, Yank. You an' me'd best be goin' to give 'em a hand wid their truck. 'Twill put 'em in good spirits.

COCKY — [*As they start off left.*] Ho, you ain't 'arf a fox, Drisc. Down't drink it all afore we sees it.

DRISCOLL — [*Over his shoulder.*] You'll be havin' yours, me sonny bye, don't fret. [*He and Yank go off left.*]

COCKY — [*Licking his lips.*] Gawd blimey, I can do wiv a wet.

DAVIS — Me, too!

CHIPS — I'll bet there ain't none of us'll let any go to waste.

BIG FRANK — I could trink a whole barrel mineself, py chiminy Christmas!

COCKY — I 'opes all the gels ain't as bloomin' ugly as 'er. Looked like a bloody organ-grinder's monkey, she did. Gawd, I couldn't put up wiv the likes of 'er!

PADDY — Ye'll be lucky if any of thim looks at ye, ye squint-eyed runt.

COCKY — [*Angrily.*] Ho, yus? You ain't no bleedin' beauty prize yeself, me man. A 'airy ape, I calls yer.

PADDY — [*Walking toward him — truculently.*] Whot's thot? Say ut again if ye dare.

COCKY — [*His hand on his sheath knife — snarling.*] 'Airy ape! That's wot I says! [PADDY *tries to reach him but the others keep them apart.*]

BIG FRANK — [*Pushing* PADDY *back.*] Vot's the matter mit you, Paddy. Don't you hear vat Driscoll say — no fighting?

PADDY — [*Grumblingly.*] I don't take no back talk from that deck-scrubbin' shrimp.

COCKY — Blarsted coal-puncher! [DRISCOLL *appears wearing a broad grin of satisfaction. The fight is immediately forgotten by the crowd who gather around him with exclamations of eager curiosity.* How is it, Drisc? Any luck? Vot she bring, Drisc? Where's the gels? *etc.*]

DRISCOLL — [*With an apprehensive glance back at the bridge.*] Not so loud, for the love av hivin! [*The clamor dies down.*] Yis, she has ut wid her. She'll be here in a minute wid a pint bottle or two for each wan av ye — three shillin's a bottle. So don't be impashunt.

COCKY — [*Indignantly.*] Three bob! The bloody cow!

SMITTY — [*With an ironic smile.*] Grand larceny, by God! [*They all turn and look up at him, surprised to hear him speak.*]

OLSON — Py yingo, we don't pay so much.

BIG FRANK — Tamn black tief!

PADDY — We'll take ut away from her and give her nothin'.

THE CROWD — [*Growling.*] Dirty thief! Dot's right! Give her nothin'! Not a bloomin' 'apenny! etc.

DRISCOLL — [*Grinning.*] Ye can take ut or lave ut, me sonny byes. [*He casts a glance in the direction of the bridge and then reaches inside his shirt and pulls out a pint bottle.*] 'Tis foine rum, the rale stuff. [*He drinks.*] I slipped this wan out av wan av the baskets whin they wasn't lookin'. [*He hands the bottle to* OLSON *who is nearest him.*] Here ye are, Ollie. Take a small sup an' pass ut to the nixt. 'Tisn't much but 'twill serve to take the black taste out av your mouths if ye go aisy wid ut. An' there's buckets more av ut comin'. [*The bottle passes from hand to hand, each man taking a sip and smacking his lips with a deep "Aa-ah" of satisfaction.*]

DAVIS — Where's she now, Drisc?

DRISCOLL — Up havin' a worrd wid the skipper, makin' arrangements about the money, I s'pose.

DAVIS — An' where's the other gels?

DRISCOLL — Wid her. There's foive av thim she took aboard — two swate little slips av things, near as white as you an' me are, for that gray-whiskered auld fool, an' the mates — an' the engineers too, maybe. The rist av thim'll be comin' for'ard whin she comes.

COCKY — 'E ain't 'arf a funny ole bird, the skipper. Gawd blimey! 'Member when we sailed from 'ome 'ow 'e stands on the bridge lookin' like a bloody ole sky pilot? An' 'is missus dawn on the bloomin' dock 'owlin' fit to kill 'erself? An' 'is kids 'owlin' an' wavin' their 'andkerchiefs? [_With great moral indignation._] An' 'ere 'e is makin' up to a bleedin' nigger! There's a captain for yer! Gawd blimey! Bloody crab, I calls 'im!

DRISCOLL — Shut up, ye insect! Sure, it's not you should be talkin', an' you wid a woman an' childer weepin' for ye in iviry divil's port in the wide worrld, if we can believe your own tale av ut.

COCKY — [_Still indignant._] I ain't no bloomin' captain, I ain't. I ain't got no missus — reg'lar married, I means. I ain't——

BIG FRANK — [_Putting a huge paw over Cocky's mouth._] You ain't going talk so much, you hear? [COCKY _wriggles away from him._] Say, Drisc, how ve pay dis voman for booze? Ve ain't got no cash.

DRISCOLL — It's aisy enough. Each girl'll have a slip av paper wid her an' whin you buy anythin' you write ut down and the price beside ut and sign your name. If ye can't write have some one who can do ut for ye. An' rimimber this: Whin ye buy a bottle av dhrink or [_With a wink._] somethin' else forbid, ye must write down tobaccy or fruit or somethin' the loike av that. Whin she laves the skipper'll pay what's owin' on the paper an' take ut out av your pay. Is ut clear to ye now?

ALL — Yes — Clear as day — Aw right, Drisc — Righto — Sure. etc.

DRISCOLL — An' don't forgit what I said about bein' quiet wid the dhrink, or the Mate'll be down on our necks an' spile the fun. [_A chorus of assent._]

DAVIS — [_Looking aft._] Ain't this them comin'? [_They all look in that direction. The silly laughter of a woman is heard._]

DRISCOLL — Look at Yank, wud ye, wid his arrm around the middle av wan av thim. That lad's not wastin' any toime. [_The four women enter from the left, giggling and whispering to each other. The first three carry baskets on their heads. The youngest and best-looking comes last._ YANK _has his arm about her waist and is carrying her basket in his other hand. All four are distinct negro types. They wear light-colored, loose-fitting clothes and have bright bandana handkerchiefs on their heads. They put down their baskets on the hatch and sit down beside them. The men crowd around, grinning._]

BELLA — [*She is the oldest, stoutest, and homeliest of the four — grinning back at them.*] Ullo, boys.

THE OTHER GIRLS — 'Ullo, boys.

THE MEN — Hello, yourself — Evenin' — Hello — How are you? etc.

BELLA — [*Genially.*] Hope you had a nice voyage. My name's Bella, this here's Susie, yander's Violet, and her there [*Pointing to the girl with* YANK.] is Pearl. Now we all knows each other.

PADDY — [*Roughly.*] Never mind the girls. Where's the dhrink?

BELLA — [*Tartly.*] You're a hawg, ain't you? Don't talk so loud or you don't git any — you nor no man. Think I wants the ole captain to put me off the ship, do you?

YANK — Yes, nix on hollerin', you! D'yuh wanta queer all of us?

BELLA — [*Casting a quick glance over her shoulder.*] Here! Some of you big strapping boys sit back of us on the hatch there so's them officers can't see what we're doin'. [DRISCOLL *and several of the others sit and stand in back of the girls on the hatch.* BELLA *turns to* DRISCOLL.] Did you tell 'em they gotter sign for what they gits — and *how* to sign?

DRISCOLL — I did — what's your name again — oh, yis — Bella, darlin'.

BELLA — Then it's all right; but you boys has gotter go inside the fo'castle when you gits your bottle. No drinkin' out here on deck. I ain't takin' no chances. [*An impatient murmur of assent goes up from the crowd.*] Ain't that right, Mike?

DRISCOLL — Right as rain, darlin'. [BIG FRANK *leans over and says something to him in a low voice.* DRISCOLL *laughs and slaps his thigh.*] Listen, Bella, I've somethin' to ask ye for my little friend here who's bashful. Ut has to do wid the ladies so I'd best be whisperin' ut to ye meself to kape them from blushin'. [*He leans over and asks her a question.*]

BELLA — [*Firmly.*] Four shillin's.

DRISCOLL — [*Laughing.*] D'you hear that, all av ye? Four shillin's ut is.

PADDY — [*Angrily.*] To hell wid this talkin'. I want a dhrink.

BELLA — Is everything all right, Mike?

DRISCOLL — [*After a look back at the bridge.*] Sure. Let her droive!

BELLA — All right, girls. [*The girls reach down in their baskets in under the fruit which is on top and each pulls out a pint bottle. Four of the men crowd up and take the bottles.*] Fetch a light, Lamps, that's a good boy.

[LAMPS *goes to his room and returns with a candle. This is passed from one girl to another as the men sign the sheets of paper for their bottles.*] Don't you boys forget to mark down cigarettes or tobacco or fruit, remember! Three shillin's is the price. Take it into the fo'castle. For Gawd's sake, don't stand out here drinkin' in the moonlight. [*The four go into the forecastle. Four more take their places.* PADDY *plants himself in front of* PEARL *who is sitting by* YANK *with his arm still around her.*]

PADDY—[*Gruffly.*] Gimme thot! [*She holds out a bottle which he snatches from her hand. He turns to go away.*]

YANK—[*Sharply.*] Here, you! Where d'yuh get that stuff? You ain't signed for that yet.

PADDY—[*Sullenly.*] I can't write me name.

YANK—Then I'll write it for yuh. [*He takes the paper from Pearl and writes.*] There ain't goin' to be no welchin' on little Bright Eyes here— not when I'm around, see? Ain't I right, kiddo?

PEARL—[*With a grin.*] Yes, suh.

BELLA—[*Seeing all four are served.*] Take it into the fo'castle, boys. [PADDY *defiantly raises his bottle and gulps down a drink in the full moonlight.* BELLA *sees him.*] Look at 'im! Look at the dirty swine! [PADDY *slouches into the forecastle.*] Wants to git me in trouble. That settles it! We all got to git inside, boys, where we won't git caught. Come on, girls. [*The girls pick up their baskets and follow* BELLA. YANK *and* PEARL *are the last to reach the doorway. She lingers behind him, her eyes fixed on* SMITTY, *who is still sitting on the forecastle head, his chin on his hands, staring off into vacancy.*]

PEARL—[*Waving a hand to attract his attention.*] Come ahn in, pretty boy. Ah likes you.

SMITTY—[*Coldly.*] Yes; I want to buy a bottle, please. [*He goes down the steps and follows her into the forecastle. No one remains on deck but* THE DONKEYMAN, *who sits smoking his pipe in front of his door. There is the subdued babble of voices from the crowd inside but the mournful cadence of the song from the shore can again be faintly heard.* SMITTY *reappears and closes the door to the forecastle after him. He shudders and shakes his shoulders as if flinging off something which disgusted him. Then he lifts the bottle which is in his hand to his lips and gulps down a long drink.* THE DONKEYMAN *watches him impassively.* SMITTY *sits down on the hatch facing him. Now that the closed door has shut off nearly all the noise the singing from shore comes clearly over the moonlit water.*]

SMITTY — [*Listening to it for a moment.*] Damn that song of theirs. [*He takes another big drink.*] What do you say, Donk?

THE DONKEYMAN — [*Quietly.*] Seems nice an' sleepy-like.

SMITTY — [*With a hard laugh.*] Sleepy! If I listened to it long — sober — I'd never go to sleep.

THE DONKEYMAN — 'Tain't sich bad music, is it? Sounds kinder pretty to me — low an' mournful — same as listenin' to the organ outside o' church of a Sunday.

SMITTY — [*With a touch of impatience.*] I didn't mean it was bad music. It isn't. It's the beastly memories the damn thing brings up — for some reason. [*He takes another pull at the bottle.*]

THE DONKEYMAN — Ever hear it before?

SMITTY — No; never in my life. It's just a something about the rotten thing which makes me think of — well — oh, the devil! [*He forces a laugh.*]

THE DONKEYMAN — [*Spitting placidly.*] Queer things, mem'ries. I ain't ever been bothered much by 'em.

SMITTY — [*Looking at him fixedly for a moment — with quiet scorn.*] No, you wouldn't be.

THE DONKEYMAN — Not that I ain't had my share o' things goin' wrong; but I puts 'em out o' me mind, like, an' fergets 'em.

SMITTY — But suppose you couldn't put them out of your mind? Suppose they haunted you when you were awake and when you were asleep — what then?

THE DONKEYMAN — [*Quietly.*] I'd git drunk, same's you're doin'.

SMITTY — [*With a harsh laugh.*] Good advice. [*He takes another drink. He is beginning to show the effects of the liquor. His face is flushed and he talks rather wildly.*] We're poor little lambs who have lost our way, eh, Donk? Damned from here to eternity, what? God have mercy on such as we! True, isn't it, Donk?

THE DONKEYMAN — Maybe; I dunno. [*After a slight pause.*] Whatever set you goin' to sea? You ain't made for it.

SMITTY — [*Laughing wildly.*] My old friend in the bottle here, Donk.

THE DONKEYMAN — I done my share o' drinkin' in my time. [*Regretfully.*] Them was good times, those days. Can't hold up under drink no more. Doctor told me I'd got to stop or die. [*He spits contentedly.*] So I stops.

SMITTY — [*With a foolish smile.*] Then I'll drink one for you. Here's your health, old top! [*He drinks.*]

THE DONKEYMAN — [*After a pause.*] S'pose there's a gel mixed up in it someplace, ain't there?

SMITTY — [*Stiffly.*] What makes you think so?

THE DONKEYMAN — Always is when a man lets music bother 'im. [*After a few puffs at his pipe.*] An' she said she threw you over 'cause you was drunk; an' you said you was drunk 'cause she threw you over. [*He spits leisurely.*] Queer thing, love, ain't it?

SMITTY — [*Rising to his feet with drunken dignity.*] I'll trouble you not to pry into my affairs, Donkeyman.

THE DONKEYMAN — [*Unmoved.*] That's everybody's affair, what I said. I been through it many's the time. [*Genially.*] I always hit 'em a whack on the ear an' went out and got drunker'n ever. When I come home again they always had somethin' special nice cooked fur me to eat. [*Puffing at his pipe.*] That's the on'y way to fix 'em when they gits on their high horse. I don't s'pose you ever tried that?

SMITTY — [*Pompously.*] Gentlemen don't hit women.

THE DONKEYMAN — [*Placidly.*] No; that's why they has mem'ries when they hears music. [SMITTY *does not deign to reply to this but sinks into a scornful silence.* DAVIS *and the girl* VIOLET *come out of the forecastle and close the door behind them. He is staggering a bit and she is laughing shrilly.*]

DAVIS — [*Turning to the left.*] This way, Rose, or Pansy, or Jessamine, or black Tulip, or Violet, or whatever the hell flower your name is. No one'll see us back here. [*They go off left.*]

THE DONKEYMAN — There's love at first sight for you — an' plenty more o' the same in the fo'c's'tle. No mem'ries jined with that.

SMITTY — [*Really repelled.*] Shut up, Donk. You're disgusting. [*He takes a long drink.*]

THE DONKEYMAN — [*Philosophically.*] All depends on how you was brung up, I s'pose. [PEARL *comes out of the forecastle. There is a roar of voices from inside. She shuts the door behind her, sees* SMITTY *on the hatch, and comes over and sits beside him and puts her arm over his shoulder.*]

THE DONKEYMAN — [*Chuckling.*] There's love for you, Duke.

Pearl — [*Patting* Smitty's *face with her hand.*] 'Ullo, pretty boy. [Smitty *pushes her hand away coldly.*] What you doin' out here all alone by yourself?

Smitty — [*With a twisted grin.*] Thinking and, — [*He indicates the bottle in his hand.*] — drinking to stop thinking. [*He drinks and laughs maudlinly. The bottle is three-quarters empty.*]

Pearl — You oughtn't drink so much, pretty boy. Don' you know dat? You have big, big headache come mawnin'.

Smitty — [*Dryly.*] Indeed?

Pearl — Tha's true. Ah knows what Ah say. [*Cooingly.*] Why you run 'way from me, pretty boy? Ah likes you. Ah don' like them other fellahs. They act too rough. You ain't rough. You're a genelman. Ah knows. Ah can tell a genelman fahs Ah can see 'im.

Smitty — Thank you for the compliment; but you're wrong, you see. I'm merely — a ranker. [*He adds bitterly.*] And a rotter.

Pearl — [*Patting his arm.*] No, you ain't. Ah knows better. You're a genelman. [*Insinuatingly.*] Ah wouldn't have nothin' to do with them other men, but [*She smiles at him enticingly.*] you is diff'rent. [*He pushes her away from him disgustedly. She pouts.*] Don' you like me, pretty boy?

Smitty — [*A bit ashamed.*] I beg your pardon. I didn't mean to be rude, you know, really. [*His politeness is drunkenly exaggerated.*] I'm a bit off color.

Pearl — [*Brightening up.*] Den you do like me — little ways?

Smitty — [*Carelessly.*] Yes, yes, why shouldn't I? [*He suddenly laughs wildly and puts his arm around her waist and presses her to him.*] Why not? [*He pulls his arm back quickly with a shudder of disgust, and takes a drink.* Pearl *looks at him curiously, puzzled by his strange actions. The door from the forecastle is kicked open and* Yank *comes out. The uproar of shouting, laughing and singing voices has increased in violence.* Yank *staggers over toward* Smitty *and* Pearl.]

Yank — [*Blinking at them.*] What the hell — oh, it's you, Smitty the Duke. I was goin' to turn one loose on the jaw of any guy'd cop my dame, but seein' it's you —— [*Sentimentally.*] Pals is pals and any pal of mine c'n have anythin' I got, see? [*Holding out his hand.*] Shake, Duke. [Smitty *takes his hand and he pumps it up and down.*] You'n me's frens. Ain't I right?

Smitty — Right it is, Yank. But you're wrong about this girl. She isn't with me. She was just going back to the fo'c's'tle to you. [PEARL *looks at him with hatred gathering in her eyes.*]

YANK—Tha' right?

SMITTY—On my word!

YANK—[*Grabbing her arm.*] Come on then, you, Pearl! Le's have a drink with the bunch. [*He pulls her to the entrance where she shakes off his hand long enough to turn on SMITTY furiously.*]

PEARL—You swine! You can go to hell! [*She goes in the forecastle, slamming the door.*]

THE DONKEYMAN—[*Spitting calmly.*] There's love for you. They're all the same—white, brown, yeller 'n' black. A whack on the ear's the only thing'll learn 'em. [SMITTY *makes no reply but laughs harshly and takes another drink; then sits staring before him, the almost empty bottle tightly clutched in one hand. There is an increase in volume of the muffled clamor from the forecastle and a moment later the door is thrown open and the whole mob, led by Driscoll, pours out on deck. All of them are very drunk and several of them carry bottles in their hands. BELLA is the only one of the women who is absolutely sober. She tries in vain to keep the men quiet. PEARL drinks from YANK'S bottle every moment or so, laughing shrilly, and leaning against YANK, whose arm is about her waist. PAUL comes out last carrying an accordion. He staggers over and stands on top of the hatch, his instrument under his arm.*]

DRISCOLL—Play us a dance, ye square-head swab!—a rale, Godforsaken son av a turkey trot wid guts to ut.

YANK—Straight from the old Barbary Coast in Frisco!

PAUL—I don' know. I try. [*He commences tuning up.*]

YANK—Ataboy! Let 'er rip! [DAVIS *and* VIOLET *come back and join the crowd.* THE DONKEYMAN *looks on them all with a detached, indulgent air.* SMITTY *stares before him and does not seem to know there is any one on deck but himself.*]

BIG FRANK—Dance? I don't dance. I trink! [*He suits the action to the word and roars with meaningless laughter.*]

DRISCOLL—Git out av the way thin, ye big hulk, an' give us some room. [BIG FRANK *sits down on the hatch, right. All of the others who are not going to dance either follow his example or lean against the port bulwark.*]

BELLA—[*On the verge of tears at her inability to keep them in the forecastle or make them be quiet now they are out.*] For Gawd's sake, boys, don't shout so loud! Want to git me in trouble?

DRISCOLL — [*Grabbing her.*] Dance wid me, me cannibal quane. [*Some one drops a bottle on deck and it smashes.*]

BELLA — [*Hysterically.*] There they goes! There they goes! Captain'll hear that! Oh, my Lawd!

DRISCOLL — Be damned to him! Here's the music! Off ye go! [PAUL *starts playing "You Great Big Beautiful Doll" with a note left out every now and then. The four couples commence dancing—a jerk-shouldered version of the old Turkey Trot as it was done in the sailor-town dives, made more grotesque by the fact that all the couples are drunk and keep lurching into each other every moment. Two of the men start dancing together, intentionally bumping into the others.* YANK *and* PEARL *come around in front of* SMITTY *and, as they pass him,* PEARL *slaps him across the side of the face with all her might, and laughs viciously. He jumps to his feet with his fists clenched but sees who hit him and sits down again smiling bitterly.* YANK *laughs boisterously.*]

YANK — Wow! Some wallop! One on you, Duke.

DRISCOLL — [*Hurling his cap at* PAUL.] Faster, ye toad! [PAUL *makes frantic efforts to speed up and the music suffers in the process.*]

BELLA — [*Puffing.*] Let me go. I'm wore out with you steppin' on my toes, you clumsy Mick. [*She struggles but Driscoll holds her tight.*]

DRISCOLL — God blarst you for havin' such big feet, thin. Aisy, aisy, Mrs. Old Black Joe! 'Tis dancin'll take the blubber off ye. [*He whirls her around the deck by main force.* COCKY, *with* SUSIE, *is dancing near the hatch, right, when* PADDY, *who is sitting on the edge with* BIG FRANK, *sticks his foot out and the wavering couple stumble over it and fall flat on the deck. A roar of laughter goes up.* COCKY *rises to his feet, his face livid with rage, and springs at* PADDY, *who promptly knocks him down.* DRIS-COLL *hits* PADDY *and* BIG FRANK *hits* DRISCOLL. *In a flash a wholesale fight has broken out and the deck is a surging crowd of drink-maddened men hitting out at each other indiscriminately, although the general idea seems to be a battle between seamen and firemen. The women shriek and take refuge on top of the hatch, where they huddle in a frightened group. Finally there is the flash of a knife held high in the moonlight and a loud yell of pain.*]

DAVIS — [*Somewhere in the crowd.*] Here's the Mate comin'! Let's git out o' this! [*There is a general rush for the forecastle. In a moment there is no one left on deck but the little group of women on the hatch;* SMITTY, *still dazedly rubbing his cheek;* THE DONKEYMAN *quietly smoking on his stool; and* YANK *and* DRISCOLL, *their faces battered up considerably, their undershirts in shreds, bending over the still form of* PADDY, *which lies stretched out on the deck between them. In the silence the mournful chant from the shore creeps slowly out to the ship.*]

DRISCOLL — [*Quickly — in a low voice.*] Who knoifed him?

YANK — [*Stupidly.*] I didn't see it. How do I know? Cocky, I'll bet. [*The* FIRST MATE *enters from the left. He is a tall, strongly-built man dressed in a plain blue uniform.*]

THE MATE — [*Angrily.*] What's all this noise about? [*He sees the man lying on the deck.*] Hello! What's this? [*He bends down on one knee beside* PADDY.]

DRISCOLL — [*Stammering.*] All av us — was in a bit av a harmless foight, sir, — an' — I dunno —— [THE MATE *rolls* PADDY *over and sees a knife wound on his shoulder.*]

THE MATE — Knifed, by God. [*He takes an electric flash from his pocket and examines the cut.*] Lucky it's only a flesh wound. He must have hit his head on deck when he fell. That's what knocked him out. This is only a scratch. Take him aft and I'll bandage him up.

DRISCOLL — Yis, sor. [*They take* PADDY *by the shoulders and feet and carry him off left.* THE MATE *looks up and sees the women on the hatch for the first time.*]

THE MATE — [*Surprised.*] Hello! [*He walks over to them.*] Go to the cabin and get your money and clear off. If I had my way, you'd never —— [*His foot hits a bottle. He stoops down and picks it up and smells of it.*] Rum, by God! So that's the trouble! I thought their breaths smelled damn queer. [*To the women, harshly.*] You needn't go to the skipper for any money. You won't get any. That'll teach you to smuggle rum on a ship and start a riot.

BELLA — But, Mister ——

THE MATE — [*Sternly.*] You know the agreement — rum — no money.

BELLA — [*Indignantly.*] Honest to Gawd, Mister, I never brung no ——

THE MATE — [*Fiercely.*] You're a liar! And none of your lip or I'll make a complaint ashore to-morrow and have you locked up.

BELLA — [*Subdued.*] Please, Mister ——

THE MATE — Clear out of this, now! Not another word out of you!

Tumble over the side damn quick! The two others are waiting for you. Hop, now! [*They walk quickly — almost run — off to the left.* The Mate *follows them, nodding to* The Donkeyman, *and ignoring the oblivious* Smitty.]

[*There is absolute silence on the ship for a few moments. The melancholy song of the negroes drifts crooning over the water.* Smitty *listens to it intently for a time; then sighs heavily, a sigh that is half a sob.*]

Smitty — God! [*He drinks the last drop in the bottle and throws it behind him on the hatch.*]

The Donkeyman — [*Spitting tranquilly.*] More mem'ries? [Smitty *does not answer him. The ship's bell tolls four bells.* The Donkeyman *knocks out his pipe.*] I think I'll turn in. [*He opens the door to his cabin, but turns to look at* Smitty — *kindly.*] You can't hear it in the fo'c's'tle — the music, I mean — an' there'll likely be more drink in there, too. Good night. [*He goes in and shuts the door.*]

Smitty — Good night, Donk. [*He gets wearily to his feet and walks with bowed shoulders, staggering a bit, to the forecastle entrance and goes in. There is silence for a second or so, broken only by the haunted, saddened voice of that brooding music, faint and far-off, like the mood of the moonlight made audible.*]

[*The Curtain Falls*]

Bound East for Cardiff

A PLAY IN ONE ACT

CHARACTERS

YANK
DRISCOLL
COCKY
DAVIS
SCOTTY
OLSON
PAUL
SMITTY
IVAN
THE CAPTAIN
THE SECOND MATE

SCENE — *The seamen's forecastle of the British tramp steamer* Glencairn *on a foggy night midway on the voyage between New York and Cardiff. An irregular shaped compartment, the sides of which almost meet at the far end to form a triangle. Sleeping bunks about six feet long, ranged three deep with a space of three feet separating the upper from the lower, are built against the sides. On the right above the bunks three or four port holes can be seen. In front of the bunks, rough wooden benches. Over the bunks on the left, a lamp in a bracket. In the left foreground, a doorway. On the floor near it, a pail with a tin dipper. Oilskins are hanging from a hook near the doorway.*

The far side of the forecastle is so narrow that it contains only one series of bunks.

In under the bunks a glimpse can be had of seachests, suit cases, seaboots, etc., jammed in indiscriminately.

At regular intervals of a minute or so the blast of the steamer's whistle can be heard above all the other sounds.

Five men are sitting on the benches talking. They are dressed in dirty patched suits of dungaree, flannel shirts, and all are in their stocking feet. Four of the men are pulling on pipes and the air is heavy with rancid tobacco smoke. Sitting on the top bunk in the left foreground, a Norwegian, PAUL, *is softly playing some folk song on a battered accordion. He stops from time to time to listen to the conversation.*

In the lower bunk in the rear a dark-haired, hard-featured man is lying apparently asleep. One of his arms is stretched limply over the side of the bunk. His face is very pale, and drops of clammy perspiration glisten on his forehead.

It is nearing the end of the dog watch — about ten minutes to eight in the evening.

COCKY — [*A weazened runt of a man. He is telling a story. The others are listening with amused, incredulous faces, interrupting him at the end of each sentence with loud derisive guffaws.*] Makin' love to me, she was! It's Gawd's truth! A bloomin' nigger! Greased all over with cocoanut oil, she was. Gawd blimey, I couldn't stand 'er. Bloody old cow, I says; and with that I fetched 'er a biff on the ear wot knocked 'er silly, an' —— [*He is interrupted by a roar of laughter from the others.*]

DAVIS — [*A middle-aged man with black hair and mustache.*] You're a liar, Cocky.

SCOTTY — [*A dark young fellow.*] Ho-ho! Ye werr neverr in New Guinea in yourr life, I'm thinkin'.

OLSON — [*A Swede with a drooping blond mustache — with ponderous sarcasm.*] Yust tink of it! You say she wass a cannibal, Cocky?

DRISCOLL — [*A brawny Irishman with the battered features of a prizefighter.*] How cud ye doubt ut, Ollie? A quane av the naygurs she musta been surely. Who else wud think herself aqual to fallin' in love wid a beauthiful, divil-may-care rake av a man the loike av Cocky? [*A burst of laughter from the crowd.*]

COCKY — [*Indignantly.*] Gawd strike me dead if it ain't true, every bleedin' word of it. 'Appened ten year ago come Christmas.

SCOTTY — 'Twas a Christmas dinner she had her eyes on.

DAVIS — He'd a been a tough old bird.

DRISCOLL — 'Tis lucky for both av ye ye escaped; for the quane av the cannibal isles wad 'a died av the belly ache the day afther Christmas, divil a doubt av ut. [*The laughter at this is long and loud.*]

COCKY — [*Sullenly.*] Blarsted fat 'eads! [*The sick man in the lower bunk in the rear groans and moves restlessly. There is a hushed silence. All the men turn and stare at him.*]

DRISCOLL — Ssshh! [*In a hushed whisper.*] We'd best not be talkin' so loud and him tryin' to have a bit av a sleep. [*He tiptoes softly to the side of the bunk.*] Yank! You'd be wantin' a drink av wather, maybe? [YANK *does not reply.* DRISCOLL *bends over and looks at him.*] It's asleep he is, sure enough. His breath is chokin' in his throat loike wather gurglin' in a poipe. [*He comes back quietly and sits down. All are silent, avoiding each other's eyes.*]

COCKY — [*After a pause.*] Pore devil! It's over the side for 'im, Gawd 'elp 'im.

DRISCOLL — Stop your croakin'! He's not dead yet and, praise God, he'll have many a long day yet before him.

SCOTTY — [*Shaking his head doubtfully.*] He's bod, mon, he's verry bod.

DAVIS — Lucky he's alive. Many a man's light woulda gone out after a fall like that.

OLSON — You saw him fall?

DAVIS — Right next to him. He and me was goin' down in number two hold to do some chippin'. He puts his leg over careless-like and misses the ladder and plumps straight down to the bottom. I was scared to look over for a minute, and then I heard him groan and I scuttled down after him. He was hurt bad inside for the blood was drippin' from the side of his mouth. He was groanin' hard, but he never let a word out of him.

COCKY — An' you blokes remember when we 'auled 'im in 'ere? Oh, 'ell, 'e says, oh, 'ell — like that, and nothink else.

OLSON — Did the captain know where he iss hurted?

COCKY — That silly ol' josser! Wot the 'ell would 'e know abaht anythink?

SCOTTY — [*Scornfully.*] He fiddles in his mouth wi' a bit of glass.

DRISCOLL — [*Angrily.*] The divil's own life ut is to be out on the lonely sea wid nothin' betune you and a grave in the ocean but a spindle-shanked, gray-whiskered auld fool the loike av him. 'Twas enough to make a saint shwear to see him wid his gold watch in his hand, tryin' to look as wise as an owl on a tree, and all the toime he not knowin' whether 'twas cholery or the barber's itch was the matther wid Yank.

SCOTTY — [*Sardonically.*] He gave him a dose of salts, na doot?

DRISCOLL — Divil a thing he gave him at all, but looked in the book he had wid him, and shook his head, and walked out widout sayin' a word, the second mate afther him no wiser than himself, God's curse on the two av thim!

COCKY — [*After a pause.*] Yank was a good shipmate, pore beggar. Lend me four bob in Noo Yark, 'e did.

DRISCOLL — [*Warmly.*] A good shipmate he was and is, none betther. Ye said no more than the truth, Cocky. Five years and more ut is since first I shipped wid him, and we've stuck together iver since through good luck and bad. Fights we've had, God help us, but 'twas only when we'd a bit av drink taken, and we always shook hands the nixt mornin'. What-iver was his was mine, and many's the toime I'd a been on the beach or worse, but for him. And now — [*His voice trembles as he fights to control his emotion.*] Divil take me if I'm not startin' to blubber loike an auld woman, and he not dead at all, but goin' to live many a long year yet, maybe.

DAVIS — The sleep'll do him good. He seems better now.

OLSON — If he wude eat someting —

DRISCOLL — Wud ye have him be eatin' in his condishun? Sure it's hard enough on the rest av us wid nothin' the matther wid our insides to be stomachin' the skoff on this rusty lime-juicer.

SCOTTY — [*Indignantly.*] It's a starvation ship.

DAVIS — Plenty o' work and no food — and the owners ridin' around in carriages!

OLSON — Hash, hash! Stew, stew! Marmalade, py damn! [*He spits disgustedly.*]

COCKY — Bloody swill! Fit only for swine is wot I say.

DRISCOLL — And the dishwather they disguise wid the name av tea! And the putty they call bread! My belly feels loike I'd swalleyed a dozen rivets at the thought av ut! And sea-biscuit that'd break the teeth av a lion if he had the misfortune to take a bite at one! [*Unconsciously they have all raised their voices, forgetting the sick man in their sailor's delight at finding something to grumble about.*]

PAUL — [*Swings his feet over the side of his bunk, stops playing his accordion, and says slowly*]: And rot-ten po-tay-toes! [*He starts in playing again. The sick man gives a groan of pain.*]

DRISCOLL — [*Holding up his hand.*] Shut your mouths, all av you. 'Tis a hell av a thing for us to be complainin' about our guts, and a sick man maybe dyin' listenin' to us. [*Gets up and shakes his fist at the Norwegian.*] God stiffen you, ye square-head scut! Put down that organ av yours or I'll break your ugly face for you. Is that banshee schreechin' fit music for a sick man? [*The Norwegian puts his accordion in the bunk and lies back and closes his eyes. DRISCOLL goes over and stands beside YANK. The steamer's whistle sounds particularly loud in the silence.*]

DAVIS — Damn this fog! [*Reaches in under a bunk and yanks out a pair of seaboots, which he pulls on.*] My lookout next, too. Must be nearly eight bells, boys. [*With the exception of* OLSON, *all the men sitting up put on oilskins, sou'westers, seaboots, etc., in preparation for the watch on deck. Olson crawls into a lower bunk on the right.*]

SCOTTY — My wheel.

OLSON — [*Disgustedly.*] Nothin' but yust dirty weather all dis voyage. I yust can't sleep when weestle blow. [*He turns his back to the light and is soon fast asleep and snoring.*]

SCOTTY — If this fog keeps up, I'm tellin' ye, we'll no be in Carrdiff for a week or more.

DRISCOLL — 'Twas just such a night as this the auld Dover wint down. Just about this toime ut was, too, and we all sittin' round in the fo'castle, Yank beside me, whin all av a suddint we heard a great slitherin' crash, and the ship heeled over till we was all in a heap on wan side. What came afther I disremimber exactly, except 'twas a hard shift to get the boats over the side before the auld teakittle sank. Yank was in the same boat wid me, and sivin morthal days we drifted wid scarcely a drop of wather or a bite to chew on. 'Twas Yank here that held me down whin I wanted to jump into the ocean, roarin' mad wid the thirst. Picked up we were on the same day wid only Yank in his senses, and him steerin' the boat.

COCKY — [*Protestingly.*] Blimey but you're a cheerful blighter, Driscoll! Talkin' abaht shipwrecks in this 'ere blushin' fog. [YANK *groans and stirs uneasily, opening his eyes.* DRISCOLL *hurries to his side.*]

DRISCOLL — Are ye feelin' any betther, Yank?

YANK — [*In a weak voice.*] No.

DRISCOLL — Sure, you must be. You look as sthrong as an ox. [*Appealing to the others.*] Am I tellin' him a lie?

DAVIS — The sleep's done you good.

COCKY — You'll be 'avin your pint of beer in Cardiff this day week.

SCOTTY — And fish and chips, mon!

YANK — [*Peevishly.*] What're yuh all lyin' fur? D'yuh think I'm scared to — [*He hesitates as if frightened by the word he is about to say.*]

DRISCOLL — Don't be thinkin' such things! [*The ship's bell is heard heavily tolling eight times. From the forecastle head above the voice of the lookout rises in a long wail:* Aaall's welll. *The men look uncertainly at* YANK *as if undecided whether to say good-by or not.*]

YANK—[*In an agony of fear.*] Don't leave me, Drisc! I'm dyin', I tell yuh. I won't stay here alone with every one snorin'. I'll go out on deck. [*He makes a feeble attempt to rise, but sinks back with a sharp groan. His breath comes in wheezy gasps.*] Don't leave me, Drisc! [*His face grows white and his head falls back with a jerk.*]

DRISCOLL—Don't be worryin', Yank. I'll not move a step out av here—and let that divil av a bosun curse his black head off. You speak a word to the bosun, Cocky. Tell him that Yank is bad took and I'll be stayin' wid him a while yet.

COCKY—Right-o. [COCKY, DAVIS, *and* SCOTTY *go out quietly.*]

COCKY—[*From the alleyway.*] Gawd blimey, the fog's thick as soup.

DRISCOLL—Are ye satisfied now, Yank? [*Receiving no answer, he bends over the still form.*] He's fainted, God help him! [*He gets a tin dipper from the bucket and bathes* YANK'S *forehead with the water.* YANK *shudders and opens his eyes.*]

YANK—[*Slowly.*] I thought I was goin' then. Wha' did yuh wanta wake me up fur?

DRISCOLL—[*With forced gayety.*] Is it wishful for heaven ye are?

YANK—[*Gloomily.*] Hell, I guess.

DRISCOLL—[*Crossing himself involuntarily.*] For the love av the saints don't be talkin' loike that! You'd give a man the creeps. It's chippin' rust on deck you'll be in a day or two wid the best av us. [YANK *does not answer, but closes his eyes wearily. The seaman who has been on lookout,* SMITTY, *a young Englishman, comes in and takes off his dripping oilskins. While he is doing this the man whose turn at the wheel has been relieved enters. He is a dark burly fellow with a round stupid face. The Englishman steps softly over to* DRISCOLL. *The other crawls into a lower bunk.*]

SMITTY—[*Whispering.*] How's Yank?

DRISCOLL—Bether. Ask him yourself. He's awake.

YANK—I'm all right, Smitty.

SMITTY—Glad to hear it, Yank. [*He crawls to an upper bunk and is soon asleep.*]

IVAN—[*The stupid-faced seaman who came in after* SMITTY *twists his head in the direction of the sick man.*] You feel gude, Jank?

YANK—[*Wearily.*] Yes, Ivan.

IVAN—Dot's gude. [*He rolls over on his side and falls asleep immediately.*]

YANK — [*After a pause broken only by snores — with a bitter laugh.*] Good-by and good luck to the lot of you!

DRISCOLL — Is ut painin' you again?

YANK — It hurts like hell — here. [*He points to the lower part of his chest on the left side.*] I guess my old pump's busted. Ooohh! [*A spasm of pain contracts his pale features. He presses his hand to his side and writhes on the thin mattress of his bunk. The perspiration stands out in beads on his forehead.*]

DRISCOLL — [*Terrified.*] Yank! Yank! What is ut? [*Jumping to his feet.*] I'll run for the captain. [*He starts for the doorway.*]

YANK — [*Sitting up in his bunk, frantic with fear.*] Don't leave me, Drisc! For God's sake don't leave me alone! [*He leans over the side of his bunk and spits.* DRISCOLL *comes back to him.*] Blood! Ugh!

DRISCOLL — Blood again! I'd best be gettin' the captain.

YANK — No, no, don't leave me! If yuh do I'll git up and follow you. I ain't no coward, but I'm scared to stay here with all of them asleep and snorin'. [DRISCOLL, *not knowing what to do, sits down on the bench beside him. He grows calmer and sinks back on the mattress.*] The captain can't do me no good, yuh know it yourself. The pain ain't so bad now, but I thought it had me then. It was like a buzz-saw cuttin' into me.

DRISCOLL — [*Fiercely.*] God blarst ut!

[THE CAPTAIN *and* THE SECOND MATE *of the steamer enter the forecastle.* THE CAPTAIN *is an old man with gray mustache and whiskers.* THE MATE *is clean-shaven and middle-aged. Both are dressed in simple blue uniforms.*]

THE CAPTAIN — [*Taking out his watch and feeling* YANK'S *pulse.*] And how is the sick man?

YANK — [*Feebly.*] All right, sir.

THE CAPTAIN — And the pain in the chest?

YANK — It still hurts, sir, worse than ever.

THE CAPTAIN — [*Taking a thermometer from his pocket and putting it into* YANK'S *mouth.*] Here. Be sure and keep this in under your tongue, not over it.

THE MATE — [*After a pause.*] Isn't this your watch on deck, Driscoll?

DRISCOLL — Yes, sorr, but Yank was fearin' to be alone, and —

THE CAPTAIN — That's all right, Driscoll.

DRISCOLL — Thank ye, sorr.

THE CAPTAIN — [*Stares at his watch for a moment or so; then takes the thermometer from* YANK'S *mouth and goes to the lamp to read it. His expression grows very grave. He beckons* THE MATE *and* DRISCOLL *to the corner near the doorway.* YANK *watches them furtively.* THE CAPTAIN *speaks in a low voice to* THE MATE.] Way up, both of them. [*To* DRISCOLL]: Has he been spitting blood again?

DRISCOLL — Not much for the hour just past, sorr, but before that ——

THE CAPTAIN — A great deal?

DRISCOLL — Yes, sorr.

THE CAPTAIN — He hasn't eaten anything?

DRISCOLL — No, sorr.

THE CAPTAIN — Did he drink that medicine I sent him?

DRISCOLL — Yes, sorr, but it didn't stay down.

THE CAPTAIN — [*Shaking his head.*] I'm afraid — he's very weak. I can't do anything else for him. It's too serious for me. If this had only happened a week later we'd be in Cardiff in time to ——

DRISCOLL — Plaze help him some way, sorr!

THE CAPTAIN — [*Impatiently.*] But, my good man, I'm not a doctor. [*More kindly as he sees* DRISCOLL'S *grief.*] You and he have been shipmates a long time?

DRISCOLL — Five years and more, sorr.

THE CAPTAIN — I see. Well, don't let him move. Keep him quiet and we'll hope for the best. I'll read the matter up and send him some medicine, something to ease the pain, anyway. [*Goes over to* YANK.] Keep up your courage! You'll be better to-morrow. [*He breaks down lamely before* YANK'S *steady gaze.*] We'll pull you through all right — and — hm — well — coming, Robinson? Dammit! [*He goes out hurriedly, followed by* THE MATE.]

DRISCOLL — [*Trying to conceal his anxiety.*] Didn't I tell you you wasn't half as sick as you thought you was? The Captain'll have you out on deck cursin' and swearin' loike a trooper before the week is out.

YANK — Don't lie, Drisc. I heard what he said, and if I didn't I c'd tell by the way I feel. I know what's goin' to happen. I'm goin' to —— [*He hesitates for a second — then resolutely.*] I'm goin' to die, that's what, and the sooner the better!

DRISCOLL — [*Wildly.*] No, and be damned to you, you're not. I'll not let you.

YANK — It ain't no use, Drisc. I ain't got a chance, but I ain't scared. Gimme a drink of water, will yuh, Drisc? My throat's burnin' up.

[DRISCOLL *brings the dipper full of water and supports his head while he drinks in great gulps.*]

DRISCOLL — [*Seeking vainly for some word of comfort.*] Are ye feelin' more aisy loike now?

YANK — Yes — now — when I know it's all up. [*A pause.*] You mustn't take it so hard, Drisc. I was just thinkin' it ain't as bad as people think — dyin'. I ain't never took much stock in the truck them sky-pilots preach. I ain't never had religion; but I know whatever it is what comes after it can't be no worser'n this. I don't like to leave you, Drisc, but — that's all.

DRISCOLL — [*With a groan.*] Lad, lad, don't be talkin'.

YANK — This sailor life ain't much to cry about leavin' — just one ship after another, hard work, small pay, and bum grub; and when we git into port, just a drunk endin' up in a fight, and all your money gone, and then ship away again. Never meetin' no nice people; never gittin outa sailor town, hardly, in any port; travellin' all over the world and never seein' none of it; without no one to care whether you're alive or dead. [*With a bitter smile.*] There ain't much in all that that'd make yuh sorry to lose it, Drisc.

DRISCOLL — [*Gloomily.*] It's a hell av a life, the sea.

YANK — [*Musingly.*] It must be great to stay on dry land all your life and have a farm with a house of your own with cows and pigs and chickens, 'way in the middle of the land where yuh'd never smell the sea or see a ship. It must be great to have a wife, and kids to play with at night after supper when your work was done. It must be great to have a home of your own, Drisc.

DRISCOLL — [*With a great sigh.*] It must, surely; but what's the use av thinkin' av ut? Such things are not for the loikes av us.

YANK — Sea-farin' is all right when you're young and don't care, but we ain't chickens no more, and somehow, I dunno, this last year has seemed rotten, and I've had a hunch I'd quit — with you, of course — and we'd save our coin, and go to Canada or Argentine or some place and git a farm, just a small one, just enough to live on. I never told yuh this cause I thought you'd laugh at me.

DRISCOLL — [*Enthusiastically.*] Laugh at you, is ut? When I'm havin' the same thoughts myself, toime afther toime. It's a grand idea and we'll be doin' ut sure if you'll stop your crazy notions — about — about bein' so sick.

YANK — [*Sadly.*] Too late. We shouldn'ta made this trip, and then —— How'd all the fog git in here?

DRISCOLL — Fog?

YANK — Everything looks misty. Must be my eyes gittin' weak, I guess. What was we talkin' of a minute ago? Oh, yes, a farm. It's too late. [*His mind wandering.*] Argentine, did I say? D'yuh remember the times we've had in Buenos Aires? The moving pictures in Barracas? Some class to them, d'yuh remember?

DRISCOLL — [*With satisfaction.*] I do that; and so does the piany player. He'll not be forgettin' the black eye I gave him in a hurry.

YANK — Remember the time we was there on the beach and had to go to Tommy Moore's boarding house to git shipped? And he sold us rotten oilskins and seaboots full of holes, and shipped us on a skysail yarder round the Horn, and took two months' pay for it. And the days we used to sit on the park benches along the Paseo Colon with the vigilantes lookin' hard at us? And the songs at the Sailor's Opera where the guy played ragtime — d'yuh remember them?

DRISCOLL — I do, surely.

YANK — And La Plata — phew, the stink of the hides! I always liked Argentine — all except that booze, caña. How drunk we used to git on that, remember?

DRISCOLL — Cud I forget ut? My head pains me at the menshun av that divil's brew.

YANK — Remember the night I went crazy with the heat in Singapore? And the time you was pinched by the cops in Port Said? And the time we was both locked up in Sydney for fightin'?

DRISCOLL — I do so.

YANK — And that fight on the dock at Cape Town —— [*His voice betrays great inward perturbation.*]

DRISCOLL — [*Hastily.*] Don't be thinkin' av that now. 'Tis past and gone.

YANK — D'yuh think He'll hold it up against me?

DRISCOLL — [*Mystified.*] Who's that?

YANK — God. They say He sees everything. He must know it was done in fair fight, in self-defense, don't yuh think?

DRISCOLL — Av course. Ye stabbed him, and be damned to him, for the skulkin' swine he was, afther him tryin' to stick you in the back, and you not suspectin'. Let your conscience be aisy. I wisht I had nothin' blacker than that on my sowl. I'd not be afraid av the angel Gabriel himself.

YANK — [*With a shudder.*] I c'd see him a minute ago with the blood spurtin' out of his neck. Ugh!

DRISCOLL — The fever, ut is, that makes you see such things. Give no heed to ut.

YANK — [*Uncertainly.*] You don't think He'll hold it up agin me — God, I mean.

DRISCOLL — If there's justice in hiven, no! [YANK *seems comforted by this assurance.*]

YANK — [*After a pause.*] We won't reach Cardiff for a week at least. I'll be buried at sea.

DRISCOLL — [*Putting his hands over his ears.*] Ssshh! I won't listen to you.

YANK — [*As if he had not heard him.*] It's as good a place as any other, I s'pose — only I always wanted to be buried on dry land. But what the hell'll I care — then? [*Fretfully.*] Why should it be a rotten night like this with that damned whistle blowin' and people snorin' all round? I wish the stars was out, and the moon, too; I c'd lie out on deck and look at them, and it'd make it easier to go — somehow.

DRISCOLL — For the love av God don't be talkin' loike that!

YANK — Whatever pay's comin' to me yuh can divvy up with the rest of the boys; and you take my watch. It ain't worth much, but it's all I've got.

DRISCOLL — But have ye no relations at all to call your own?

YANK — No, not as I know of. One thing I forgot: You know Fanny the barmaid at the Red Stork in Cardiff?

DRISCOLL — Sure, and who doesn't?

YANK — She's been good to me. She tried to lend me half a crown when I was broke there last trip. Buy her the biggest box of candy yuh c'n find in Cardiff. [*Breaking down — in a choking voice.*] It's hard to ship on this voyage I'm goin' on — alone! [DRISCOLL *reaches out and grasps his hand. There is a pause, during which both fight to control themselves.*] My throat's like a furnace. [*He gasps for air.*] Gimme a drink of water, will yuh, Drisc? [DRISCOLL *gets him a dipper of water.*] I wish this was a pint of beer. Oooohh! [*He chokes, his face convulsed with agony, his hands tearing at his shirt front. The dipper falls from his nerveless fingers.*]

DRISCOLL — For the love av God, what is ut, Yank?

YANK — [*Speaking with tremendous difficulty.*] S'long, Drisc! [*He stares straight in front of him with eyes starting from their sockets.*] Who's that?

DRISCOLL — Who? What?

YANK — [*Faintly.*] A pretty lady dressed in black. [*His face twitches and his body writhes in a final spasm, then straightens out rigidly.*]

DRISCOLL — [*Pale with horror.*] Yank! Yank! Say a word to me for the love av hiven! [*He shrinks away from the bunk, making the sign of the cross. Then comes back and puts a trembling hand on* YANK'S *chest and bends closely over the body.*]

COCKY — [*From the alleyway.*] Oh, Driscoll! Can you leave Yank for arf a mo' and give me a 'and?

DRISCOLL — [*With a great sob.*] Yank! [*He sinks down on his knees beside the bunk, his head on his hands. His lips move in some half-remembered prayer.*]

COCKY — [*Enters, his oilskins and sou'wester glistening with drops of water.*] The fog's lifted. [COCKY *sees* DRISCOLL *and stands staring at him with open mouth.* DRISCOLL *makes the sign of the cross again.*]

COCKY — [*Mockingly.*] Sayin' 'is prayers! [*He catches sight of the still figure in the bunk and an expression of awed understanding comes over his face. He takes off his dripping sou'wester and stands, scratching his head.*]

COCKY — [*In a hushed whisper.*] Gawd blimey!

[*The Curtain Falls*]

The Long Voyage Home

A PLAY IN ONE ACT

CHARACTERS

FAT JOE, *proprietor of a dive.*
NICK, *a crimp.*
MAG, *a barmaid.*
OLSON ⎤
DRISCOLL ⎟ *Seamen of the British tramp steamer,*
COCKY ⎟   Glencairn.
IVAN ⎦
KATE
FREDA
TWO ROUGHS

SCENE—*The bar of a low dive on the London waterfront—a squalid, dingy room dimly lighted by kerosene lamps placed in brackets on the walls. On the left, the bar. In front of it, a door leading to a side room. On the right, tables with chairs around them. In the rear, a door leading to the street.*

A slovenly barmaid with a stupid face sodden with drink is mopping off the bar. Her arm moves back and forth mechanically and her eyes are half shut as if she were dozing on her feet. At the far end of the bar stands FAT JOE, *the proprietor, a gross bulk of a man with an enormous stomach. His face is red and bloated, his little piggish eyes being almost concealed by rolls of fat. The thick fingers of his big hands are loaded with cheap rings and a gold watch chain of cablelike proportions stretches across his checked waistcoat.*

At one of the tables, front, a round-shouldered young fellow is sitting, smoking a cigarette. His face is pasty, his mouth weak, his eyes shifting and cruel. He is dressed in a shabby suit, which must have once been cheaply flashy, and wears a muffler and cap.

It is about nine o'clock in the evening.

JOE—[*Yawning.*] Blimey if bizness ain't 'arf slow to-night. I donnow wot's 'appened. The place is like a bleedin' tomb. Where's all the sailor men, I'd like to know? [*Raising his voice.*] Ho, you Nick! [NICK *turns around listlessly.*] Wot's the name o' that wessel put in at the dock below jest arter noon?

NICK—[*Laconically.*] *Glencairn*—from Bewnezerry. [Buenos Aires].

37

JOE—Ain't the crew been paid orf yet?

NICK—Paid orf this arternoon, they tole me. I 'opped on board of 'er an' seen 'em. 'Anded 'em some o' yer cards, I did. They promised faithful they'd 'appen in to-night—them as whose time was done.

JOE—Any two-year men to be paid orf?

NICK—Four—three Britishers an' a square-'ead.

JOE—[*Indignantly.*] An' yer popped orf an' left 'em? An' me a-payin' yer to 'elp an' bring 'em in 'ere!

NICK—[*Grumblingly.*] Much you pays me! An' I ain't slingin' me 'ook abaht the 'ole bleedin' town fur now man. See?

JOE—I ain't speakin' on'y fur meself. Down't I always give yer yer share, fair an' square, as man to man?

NICK—[*With a sneer.*] Yus—b'cause you 'as to.

JOE—'As to? Listen to 'im! There's many'd be 'appy to 'ave your berth, me man!

NICK—Yus? Wot wiv the peelers li'ble to put me away in the bloody jail fur crimpin', an' all?

JOE—[*Indignantly.*] We down't do no crimpin'.

NICK—[*Sarcastically.*] Ho, now! Not arf!

JOE—[*A bit embarrassed.*] Well, on'y a bit now an' agen when there ain't no reg'lar trade. [*To hide his confusion he turns to the barmaid angrily. She is still mopping off the bar, her chin on her breast, half-asleep.*] 'Ere, me gel, we've 'ad enough o' that. You been a-moppin', an' a-moppin', an' a-moppin' the blarsted bar fur a 'ole 'our. 'Op it aht o' this! You'd fair guv a bloke the shakes a-watchin' yer.

MAG—[*Beginning to sniffle.*] Ow, you do frighten me when you 'oller at me, Joe. I ain't a bad gel, I ain't. Gawd knows I tries to do me best fur you. [*She bursts into a tempest of sobs.*]

JOE—[*Roughly.*] Stop yer grizzlin'! An' 'op it aht of 'ere!

NICK—[*Chuckling.*] She's drunk, Joe. Been 'ittin' the gin, eh, Mag?

MAG—[*Ceases crying at once and turns on him furiously.*] You little crab, you! Orter wear a muzzle, you ort! A-openin' of your ugly mouth to a 'onest woman what ain't never done you no 'arm. [*Commencing to sob again.*] H'abusin' me like a dawg cos I'm sick an' orf me oats, an' all.

JOE—Orf yer go, me gel! Go hupstairs and 'ave a sleep. I'll wake yer if I wants yer. An' wake the two gels when yer goes hup. It's 'arpas' nine an' time as some one was a-comin' in, tell 'em. D'yer 'ear me?

MAG—[*Stumbling around the bar to the door on left—sobbing.*] Yus,

yus, I 'ears you. Gawd knows wot's goin' to 'appen to me, I'm that sick. Much you cares if I dies, down't you? [*She goes out.*]

JOE — [*Still brooding over* NICK'S *lack of diligence — after a pause.*] Four two-year men paid orf wiv their bloody pockets full o' sovereigns — an' yer lorst 'em. [*He shakes his head sorrowfully.*]

NICK — [*Impatiently.*] Stow it! They promised faithful they'd come, I tells yer. They'll be walkin' in in 'arf a mo'. There's lots o' time yet. [*In a low voice.*] 'Ave yer got the drops? We might wanter use 'em.

JOE — [*Taking a small bottle from behind the bar.*] Yus; 'ere it is.

NICK — [*With satisfaction.*] Righto! [*His shifty eyes peer about the room searchingly. Then he beckons to* JOE, *who comes over to the table and sits down.*] Reason I arst yer about the drops was 'cause I seen the capt'n of the* Amindra *this arternoon.

JOE — The *Amindra*? Wot ship is that?

NICK — Bloody windjammer — skys'l yarder — full rigged — painted white — been layin' at the dock above 'ere fur a month. You knows 'er.

JOE — Ho, yus. I knows now.

NICK — The capt'n says as 'e wants a man special bad — ter-night. They sails at daybreak ter-morrer.

JOE — There's plenty o' 'ands lyin' abaht waitin' fur ships, I should fink.

NICK — Not fur this ship, ole buck. The capt'n an' mate are bloody slave-drivers, an' they're bound down round the 'Orn. They 'arf starved the 'ands on the larst trip 'ere, an' no one'll dare ship on 'er. [*After a pause.*] I promised the capt'n faithful I'd get 'im one, and ter-night.

JOE — [*Doubtfully.*] An' 'ow are yer goin' to git 'im?

NICK — [*With a wink.*] I was thinkin' as one of 'em from the *Glencairn*'d do — them as was paid orf an' is comin' 'ere.

JOE — [*With a grin.*] It'd be a good 'aul, that's the troof. [*Frowning.*] If they comes 'ere.

NICK — They'll come, an' they'll all be rotten drunk, wait an' see. [*There is the noise of loud, boisterous singing from the street.*] Sounds like 'em, now. [*He opens the street door and looks out.*] Gawd blimey if it ain't the four of 'em! [*Turning to* JOE *in triumph.*] Naw, what d'yer say? They're lookin' for the place. I'll go aht an' tell 'em. [*He goes out.* JOE *gets into position behind the bar, assuming his most oily smile. A moment later the door is opened, admitting* DRISCOLL, COCKY, IVAN *and* OLSON. DRISCOLL *is a tall, powerful Irishman*; COCKY, *a wizened runt of a man*

with a straggling gray mustache; IVAN, *a hulking oaf of a peasant;*
OLSON, *a stocky, middle-aged Swede with round, childish blue eyes. The
first three are all very drunk, especially* IVAN, *who is managing his legs
with difficulty.* OLSON *is perfectly sober. All are dressed in their ill-fitting
shore clothes and look very uncomfortable.* DRISCOLL *has unbuttoned his
stiff collar and its ends stick out sideways. He has lost his tie.* NICK *slinks
into the room after them and sits down at a table in rear. The seamen come
to the table, front.*]

JOE — [*With affected heartiness.*] Ship ahoy, mates! 'Appy to see yer
'ome safe an' sound.

DRISCOLL — [*Turns round, swaying a bit, and peers at him across the
bar.*] So ut's you, is ut? [*He looks about the place with an air of recogni-
tion.*] 'An the same damn rat's-hole, sure enough. I remimber foive or six
years back 'twas here I was sthripped av me last shillin' whin I was aslape.
[*With sudden fury.*] God stiffen ye, come none av your dog's thricks on
me this trip or I'll —— [*He shakes his fist at* JOE.]

JOE — [*Hastily interrupting.*] Yer must be mistaiken. This is a 'onest
place, this is.

COCKY — [*Derisively.*] Ho, yus! An' you're a bleedin' angel, I s'pose?

IVAN — [*Vaguely taking off his derby hat and putting it on again —
plaintively.*] I don' li-ike dis place.

DRISCOLL — [*Going over to the bar — as genial as he was furious a
moment before.*] Well, no matther, 'tis all past an' gone an' forgot. I'm not
the man to be holdin' harrd feelin's on me first night ashore, an' me
dhrunk as a lord. [*He holds out his hand, which* JOE *takes very gingerly.*]
We'll all be havin' a dhrink, I'm thinkin'. Whiskey for the three av us —
Irish whiskey!

COCKY — [*Mockingly.*] An' a glarse o' ginger beer fur our blarsted
love-child 'ere. [*He jerks his thumb at* OLSON.]

OLSON — [*With a good-natured grin.*] I bane a good boy dis night, for
one time.

DRISCOLL — [*Bellowing, and pointing to* NICK *as* JOE *brings the
drinks to the table.*] An' see what that crimpin' son av a crimp'll be
wantin' — an' have your own pleasure. [*He pulls a sovereign out of his
pocket and slams it on the bar.*]

NICK — Guv me a pint o' beer, Joe. [JOE *draws the beer and takes it
down to the far end of the bar.* NICK *comes over to get it and* JOE *gives him*

a significant wink and nods toward the door on the left. NICK *signals back that he understands.*]

COCKY — [*Drink in hand — impatiently.*] I'm that bloody dry! [*Lifting his glass to* DRISCOLL.] Cheero, ole dear, cheero!

DRISCOLL — [*Pocketing his change without looking at it.*] A toast for ye: Hell roast that divil av a bo'sun! [*He drinks.*]

COCKY — Righto! Gawd strike 'im blind! [*He drains his glass.*]

IVAN — [*Half-asleep.*] Dot's gude. [*He tosses down his drink in one gulp.* OLSON *sips his ginger ale.* NICK *takes a swallow of his beer and then comes round the bar and goes out the door on left.*]

COCKY — [*Producing a sovereign.*] Ho there, you Fatty! Guv us another!

JOE — The saime, mates?

COCKY — Yus.

DRISCOLL — No, ye scut! I'll be havin' a pint av beer. I'm dhry as a loime kiln.

IVAN — [*Suddenly getting to his feet in a befuddled manner and nearly upsetting the table.*] I don' li-ike dis place! I wan' see girls — plenty girls. [*Pathetically.*] I don't li-ike dis place. I wan' dance with girl.

DRISCOLL — [*Pushing him back on his chair with a thud.*] Shut up, ye Rooshan baboon! A foine Romeo you'd make in your condishun. [IVAN *blubbers some incoherent protest — then suddenly falls asleep.*]

JOE — [*Bringing the drinks — looks at* OLSON.] An' you, matey?

OLSON — [*Shaking his head.*] Noting dis time, thank you.

COCKY — [*Mockingly.*] A-saivin' of 'is money, 'e is! Goin' back to 'ome an' mother. Goin' to buy a bloomin' farm an' punch the blarsted dirt, that's wot 'e is! [*Spitting disgustedly.*] There's a funny bird of a sailor man for yer, Gawd blimey!

OLSON — [*Wearing the same good-natured grin.*] Yust what I like, Cocky. I wus on farm long time when I wus kid.

DRISCOLL — Lave him alone, ye bloody insect! 'Tis a foine sight to see a man wid some sense in his head instead av a damn fool the loike av us. I only wisht I'd a mother alive to call me own. I'd not be dhrunk in this divil's hole this minute, maybe.

COCKY — [*Commencing to weep dolorously.*] Ow, down't talk, Drisc! I can't bear to 'ear you. I ain't never 'ad no mother, I ain't——

DRISCOLL — Shut up, ye ape, an' don't be makin' that squealin'. If ye cud see your ugly face, wid the big red nose av ye all screwed up in a knot, ye'd never shed a tear the rist av your loife. [*Roaring into song.*] We ar-re the byes av We-e-exford who fought wid hearrt an' hand! [*Speaking.*] To hell wid Ulster! [*He drinks and the others follow his example.*] An' I'll strip to any man in the city av London won't dhrink to that toast. [*He glares truculently at* JOE, *who immediately downs his beer.* NICK *enters again from the door on the left and comes up to* JOE *and whispers in his ear. The latter nods with satisfaction.*]

DRISCOLL — [*Glowering at them.*] What divil's thrick are ye up to now, the two av ye? [*He flourishes a brawny fist.*] Play fair wid us or ye deal wid me!

JOE — [*Hastily.*] No trick, shipmate! May Gawd kill me if that ain't troof!

NICK — [*Indicating* IVAN, *who is snoring.*] On'y your mate there was arskin' fur gels an' I thorght as 'ow yer'd like 'em to come dawhn an' 'ave a wet wiv yer.

JOE — [*With a smirking wink.*] Pretty, 'olesome gels they be, ain't they, Nick?

NICK — Yus.

COCKY — Aar! I knows the gels you 'as, not 'arf! They'd fair blind yer, they're that 'omely. None of yer bloomin' gels fur me, ole Fatty. Me an' Drisc knows a place, down't we, Drisc?

DRISCOLL — Divil a lie, we do. An' we'll be afther goin' there in a minute. There's music there an' a bit av a dance to liven a man.

JOE — Nick, 'ere, can play yer a tune, can't yer, Nick?

NICK — Yus.

JOE — An' yer can 'ave a dance in the side room 'ere.

DRISCOLL — Hurroo! Now you're talkin'. [*The two women,* FREDA *and* KATE, *enter from the left.* FREDA *is a little, sallow-faced blonde.* KATE *is stout and dark.*]

COCKY — [*In a loud aside to* DRISCOLL.] Gawd blimey, look at 'em! Ain't they 'orrible? [*The women come forward to the table, wearing their best set smiles.*]

FREDA — [*In a raspy voice.*] 'Ullo, mates.

KATE — 'Ad a good voyage?

DRISCOLL — Rotten; but no matther. Welcome, as the sayin' is, an' sit down, an' what'll ye be takin' for your thirst? [*To* KATE.] You'll be sittin' by me, darlin' — what's your name?

KATE — [*With a stupid grin.*] Kate. [*She stands by his chair.*]

DRISCOLL — [*Putting his arm around her.*] A good Irish name, but you're English by the trim av ye, an' be damned to you. But no matther. Ut's fat ye are, Katy dear, an' I never cud endure skinny wimin. [FREDA *favors him with a viperish glance and sits down by* OLSON.] What'll ye have?

OLSON — No, Drisc. Dis one bane on me. [*He takes out a roll of notes from his inside pocket and lays one on the table.* JOE, NICK, *and the women look at the money with greedy eyes.* IVAN *gives a particularly violent snore.*]

FREDA — Waike up your fren'. Gawd, 'ow I 'ates to 'ear snorin'.

DRISCOLL — [*Springing to action, smashes* IVAN'S *derby over his ears.*] D'you hear the lady talkin' to ye, ye Rooshan swab? [*The only reply to this is a snore.* DRISCOLL *pulls the battered remains of the derby off* IVAN'S *head and smashes it back again.*] Arise an' shine, ye dhrunken swine! [*Another snore. The women giggle.* DRISCOLL *throws the beer left in his glass into* IVAN'S *face. The Russian comes to in a flash, spluttering. There is a roar of laughter.*]

IVAN — [*Indignantly.*] I tell you — dot's someting I don' li-ike!

COCKY — Down't waste good beer, Drisc.

IVAN — [*Grumblingly.*] I tell you — dot is not ri-ight.

DRISCOLL — Ut's your own doin', Ivan. Ye was moanin' for girrls an' whin they come you sit gruntin' loike a pig in a sty. Have ye no manners? [IVAN *seems to see the women for the first time and grins foolishly.*]

KATE — [*Laughing at him.*] Cheero, ole chum, 'ows Russha?

IVAN — [*Greatly pleased — putting his hand in his pocket.*] I buy a drink.

OLSON — No; dis one bane on me. [*To* JOE.] Hey, you faller!

JOE — Wot'll it be, Kate?

KATE — Gin.

FREDA — Brandy.

DRISCOLL — An' Irish whiskey for the rist av us — wid the excipshun av our timperance friend, God pity him!

FREDA — [*To* OLSON.] You ain't drinkin'?

OLSON — [*Half-ashamed.*] No.

FREDA — [*With a seductive smile.*] I down't blame yer. You got sense, you 'ave. I on'y tike a nip o' brandy now an' agen fur my 'ealth. [JOE *brings the drinks and* OLSON'S *change.* COCKY *gets unsteadily to his feet and raises his glass in the air.*]

COCKY—'Ere's a toff toast for yer: The ladies, Gawd—[*He hesitates—then adds in a grudging tone.*]—bless 'em.

KATE—[*With a silly giggle.*] Oo-er! That wasn't what you was goin' to say, you bad Cocky, you! [*They all drink.*]

DRISCOLL—[*To* NICK.] Where's the tune ye was promisin' to give us?

NICK—Come ahn in the side 'ere an' you'll 'ear it.

DRISCOLL—[*Getting up.*] Come on, all av ye. We'll have a tune an' a dance if I'm not too dhrunk to dance, God help me. [COCKY *and* IVAN *stagger to their feet.* IVAN *can hardly stand. He is leering at* KATE *and snickering to himself in a maudlin fashion. The three, led by* NICK, *go out the door on the left.* KATE *follows them.* OLSON *and* FREDA *remain seated.*]

COCKY—[*Calling over his shoulder.*] Come on an' dance, Ollie.

OLSON—Yes, I come. [*He starts to get up. From the side room comes the sound of an accordion and a boisterous whoop from* DRISCOLL, *followed by a heavy stamping of feet.*]

FREDA—Ow, down't go in there. Stay 'ere an' 'ave a talk wiv me. They're all drunk an' you ain't drinkin'. [*With a smile up into his face.*] I'll think yer don't like me if yer goes in there.

OLSON—[*Confused.*] You wus wrong, Miss Freda. I don't—I mean I do like you.

FREDA—[*Smiling—puts her hand over his on the table.*] An' I likes you. Yer a genelman. You don't get drunk an' hinsult poor gels wot 'as a 'ard an' uneppy life.

OLSON—[*Pleased but still more confused—wriggling his feet.*] I bane drunk many time, Miss Freda.

FREDA—Then why ain't yer drinkin' now? [*She exchanges a quick, questioning glance with* JOE, *who nods back at her—then she continues persuasively.*] Tell me somethin' abaht yeself.

OLSON—[*With a grin.*] There ain't noting to say, Miss Freda. I bane poor devil sailor man, dat's all.

FREDA—Where was you born—Norway? [OLSON *shakes his head.*] Denmark?

OLSON—No. You guess once more.

FREDA—Then it must be Sweden.

OLSON—Yes. I wus born in Stockholm.

FREDA — [*Pretending great delight.*] Ow, ain't that funny! I was born there, too — in Stockholm.

OLSON — [*Astonished.*] You wus born in Sweden?

FREDA — Yes; you wouldn't think it, but it's Gawd's troof. [*She claps her hands delightedly.*]

OLSON — [*Beaming all over.*] You speak Swedish?

FREDA — [*Trying to smile sadly.*] Now. Y'see my ole man an' woman come 'ere to England when I was on'y a baby an' they was speakin' English b'fore I was old enough to learn. Sow I never knew Swedish. [*Sadly.*] Wisht I 'ad! [*With a smile.*] We'd 'ave a bloomin' lark of it if I 'ad, wouldn't we?

OLSON — It sound nice to hear the old talk yust once in a time.

FREDA — Righto! No place like yer 'ome, I says. Are yer goin' up to — to Stockholm b'fore yer ships away agen?

OLSON — Yes. I go home from here to Stockholm. [*Proudly.*] As passenger!

FREDA — An' you'll git another ship up there arter you've 'ad a vacation?

OLSON — No. I don't never ship on sea no more. I got all sea I want for my life — too much hard work for little money. Yust work, work, work on ship. I don't want more.

FREDA — Ow, I see. That's why you give up drinkin'.

OLSON — Yes. [*With a grin.*] If I drink I yust get drunk and spend all money.

FREDA — But if you ain't gointer be a sailor no more, what'll yer do? You been a sailor all yer life, ain't yer?

OLSON — No. I work on farm till I am eighteen. I like it, too — it's nice — work on farm.

FREDA — But ain't Stockholm a city same's London? Ain't no farms there, is there?

OLSON — We live — my brother and mother live — my father iss dead — on farm yust a little way from Stockholm. I have plenty money, now. I go back with two years' pay and buy more land yet; work on farm. [*Grinning.*] No more sea, no more bum grub, no more storms — yust nice work.

FREDA — Ow, ain't that luv'ly! I s'pose you'll be gittin' married, too?

OLSON — [*Very much confused.*] I don't know. I like to, if I find nice girl, maybe.

FREDA—Ain't yer got some gel back in Stockholm? I bet yer 'as.

OLSON—No. I got nice girl once before I go on sea. But I go on ship, and I don't come back, and she marry other faller. [*He grins sheepishly.*]

FREDA—Well, it's nice for yer to be goin' 'ome, anyway.

OLSON—Yes. I tank so. [*There is a crash from the room on left and the music abruptly stops. A moment later* COCKY *and* DRISCOLL *appear, supporting the inert form of* IVAN *between them. He is in the last stage of intoxication, unable to move a muscle.* NICK *follows them and sits down at the table in rear.*]

DRISCOLL—[*As they zigzag up to the bar.*] Ut's dead he is, I'm thinkin', for he's as limp as a blarsted corpse.

COCKY—[*Puffing.*] Gawd, 'e ain't 'arf 'eavy!

DRISCOLL—[*Slapping* IVAN'S *face with his free hand.*] Wake up, ye divil, ye. Ut's no use. Gabriel's trumpet itself cudn't rouse him. [*To* JOE.] Give us a dhrink for I'm perishing wid the thirst. 'Tis harrd worrk, this.

JOE—Whiskey?

DRISCOLL—*Irish* whiskey, ye swab. [*He puts down a coin on the bar.* JOE *serves* COCKY *and* DRISCOLL. *They drink and then swerve over to* OLSON'S *table.*]

OLSON—Sit down and rest for time, Drisc.

DRISCOLL—No, Ollie, we'll be takin' this lad home to his bed. Ut's late for wan so young to be out in the night. An' I'd not trust him in this hole as dhrunk as he is, an' him wid a full pay day on him. [*Shaking his fist at* JOE.] Oho, I know your games, me sonny bye!

JOE—[*With an air of grievance.*] There yer goes again—hinsultin' a 'onest man!

COCKY—Ho, listen to 'im! Guv 'im a shove in the marf, Drisc.

OLSON—[*Anxious to avoid a fight—getting up.*] I help you take Ivan to boarding house.

FREDA—[*Protestingly.*] Ow, you ain't gointer leave me, are yer? An' we 'avin' sech a nice talk, an' all.

DRISCOLL—[*With a wink.*] Ye hear what the lady says, Ollie. Ye'd best stay here, me timperance lady's man. An' we need no help. 'Tis only a bit av a way and we're two strong men if we are dhrunk. Ut's no hard shift to take the remains home. But ye can open the door for us, Ollie. [OLSON *goes to the door and opens it.*] Come on, Cocky, an' don't be fallin' aslape yourself. [*They lurch toward the door. As they go out* DRISCOLL *shouts back over his shoulder.*] We'll be comin' back in a short time, surely. So wait here for us, Ollie.

OLSON — All right. I wait here, Drisc. [*He stands in the doorway uncertainly.* JOE *makes violent signs to* FREDA *to bring him back. She goes over and puts her arm around* OLSON'S *shoulder.* JOE *motions to* NICK *to come to the bar. They whisper together excitedly.*]

FREDA — [*Coaxingly.*] You ain't gointer leave me, are yer, dearie? [*Then irritably.*] Fur Gawd's sake, shet that door! I'm fair freezin' to death wiv the fog. [OLSON *comes to himself with a start and shuts the door.*]

OLSON — [*Humbly.*] Excuse me, Miss Freda.

FREDA — [*Leading him back to the table — coughing.*] Buy me a drink o' brandy, will yer? I'm sow cold.

OLSON — All you want, Miss Freda, all you want. [*To* JOE, *who is still whispering instructions to* NICK.] Hey, Yoe! Brandy for Miss Freda. [*He lays a coin on the table.*]

JOE — Righto! [*He pours out her drink and brings it to the table.*] 'Avin' somethink yeself, shipmate?

OLSON — No. I don't tank so. [*He points to his glass with a grin.*] Dis iss only belly-wash, no? [*He laughs.*]

JOE — [*Hopefully.*] 'Ave a man's drink.

OLSON — I would like to — but no. If I drink one I want drink one tousand. [*He laughs again.*]

FREDA — [*Responding to a vicious nudge from* JOE'S *elbow.*] Ow, tike somethin'. I ain't gointer drink all be meself.

OLSON — Den give me a little yinger beer — small one. [JOE *goes back of the bar, making a sign to* NICK *to go to their table.* NICK *does so and stands so that the sailor cannot see what* JOE *is doing.*]

NICK — [*To make talk.*] Where's yer mates popped orf ter? [JOE *pours the contents of the little bottle into* OLSON'S *glass of ginger beer.*]

OLSON — Dey take Ivan, dat drunk faller, to bed. They come back. [JOE *brings* OLSON'S *drink to the table and sets it before him.*]

JOE — [*To* NICK — *angrily.*] 'Op it, will yer? There ain't no time to be dawdlin'. See? 'Urry!

NICK — Down't worry, ole bird, I'm orf. [*He hurries out the door.* JOE *returns to his place behind the bar.*]

OLSON — [*After a pause — worriedly.*] I tank I should go after dem. Cocky iss very drunk, too, and Drisc ——

FREDA — Aar! The big Irish is all right. Don't yer 'ear 'im say as 'ow they'd surely come back 'ere, an' fur you to wait fur 'em?

OLSON — Yes; but if dey don't come soon I tank I go see if dey are in boarding house all right.

FREDA — Where is the boardin' 'ouse?

OLSON — Yust little way back from street here.

FREDA — You stayin' there, too?

OLSON — Yes — until steamer sail for Stockholm — in two day.

FREDA — [*She is alternately looking at* JOE *and feverishly trying to keep* OLSON *talking so he will forget about going away after the others.*] Yer mother won't be arf glad to see yer agen, will she? [OLSON *smiles.*] Does she know yer comin'?

OLSON — No. I tought I would yust give her surprise. I write to her from Bonos Eres but I don't tell her I come home.

FREDA — Must be old, ain't she, yer ole lady?

OLSON — She iss eighty-two. [*He smiles reminiscently.*] You know, Miss Freda, I don't see my mother or my brother in — let me tank — [*He counts laboriously on his fingers.*] must be more than ten year. I write once in while and she write many time; and my brother he write me, too. My mother say in all letter I should come home right away. My brother he write same ting, too. He want me to help him on farm. I write back always I come soon; and I mean all time to go back home at end of voyage. But I come ashore, I take one drink, I take many drinks, I get drunk, I spend all money, I have to ship away for other voyage. So dis time I say to myself: Don't drink one drink, Ollie, or, sure, you don't get home. And I want go home dis time. I feel homesick for farm and to see my people again. [*He smiles.*] Yust like little boy, I feel homesick. Dat's why I don't drink noting to-night but dis — belly-wash! [*He roars with childish laughter, then suddenly becomes serious.*] You know, Miss Freda, my mother get very old, and I want see her. She might die and I would never ——

FREDA — [*Moved a lot in spite of herself.*] Ow, don't talk like that! I jest 'ates to 'ear any one speakin' abaht dyin'. [*The door to the street is opened and* NICK *enters, followed by two rough-looking, shabbily-dressed men, wearing mufflers, with caps pulled down over their eyes. They sit at the table nearest to the door.* JOE *brings them three beers, and there is a whispered consultation, with many glances in the direction of* OLSON.]

OLSON — [*Starting to get up — worriedly.*] I tank I go round to boarding house. I tank someting go wrong with Drisc and Cocky.

FREDA — Ow, down't go. They kin take care of theyselves. They ain't babies. Wait 'arf a mo'. You ain't 'ad yer drink yet.

JOE — [*Coming hastily over to the table, indicates the men in the rear with a jerk of his thumb.*] One of them blokes wants yer to 'ave a wet wiv 'im.

FREDA — Righto! [*To* OLSON.] Let's drink this. [*She raises her glass. He does the same.*] 'Ere's a toast fur yer: Success to yer bloomin' farm an' may yer live long an' 'appy on it. Skoal! [*She tosses down her brandy. He swallows half his glass of ginger beer and makes a wry face.*]

OLSON — Skoal! [*He puts down his glass.*]

FREDA — [*With feigned indignation.*] Down't yer like my toast?

OLSON — [*Grinning.*] Yes. It iss very kind, Miss Freda.

FREDA — Then drink it all like I done.

OLSON — Well —— [*He gulps down the rest.*] Dere! [*He laughs.*]

FREDA — Done like a sport!

ONE OF THE ROUGHS — [*With a laugh.*] Amindra, ahoy!

NICK — [*Warningly.*] Sssshh!

OLSON — [*Turns around in his chair.*] Amindra? Iss she in port? I sail on her once long time ago — three mast, full rig, skys'l yarder? Iss dat ship you mean?

THE ROUGH — [*Grinning.*] Yus; right you are.

OLSON — [*Angrily.*] I know dat damn ship — worst ship dat sail to sea. Rotten grub and dey make you work all time — and the Captain and Mate wus Bluenose devils. No sailor who know anyting ever ship on her. Where iss she bound from here?

THE ROUGH — Round Cape 'Orn — sails at daybreak.

OLSON — Py yingo, I pity poor fallers make dat trip round Cape Stiff dis time year. I bet you some of dem never see port once again. [*He passes his hand over his eyes in a dazed way. His voice grows weaker.*] Py golly, I feel dizzy. All the room go round and round like I wus drunk. [*He gets weakly to his feet.*] Good night, Miss Freda. I bane feeling sick. Tell Drisc — I go home. [*He takes a step forward and suddenly collapses over a chair, rolls to the floor, and lies there unconscious.*]

JOE — [*From behind the bar.*] Quick, nawh! [NICK *darts forward with* JOE *following.* FREDA *is already beside the unconscious man and has taken the roll of money from his inside pocket. She strips off a note furtively and shoves it into her bosom, trying to conceal her action, but* JOE *sees her. She hands the roll to* JOE, *who pockets it.* NICK *goes through all the other pockets and lays a handful of change on the table.*]

JOE — [*Impatiently.*] 'Urry, 'urry, can't yer? The other blokes'll be 'ere in 'arf a mo'. [*The two roughs come forward.*] 'Ere, you two, tike 'im in under the arms like 'e was drunk. [*They do so.*] Tike 'im to the *Amindra* — yer knows that, don't yer? — two docks above. Nick'll show yer. An' you, Nick, down't yer leave the bleedin' ship till the capt'n guvs yer this bloke's advance — full month's pay — five quid, d'yer 'ear?

NICK — I knows me bizness, ole bird. [*They support* OLSON *to the door.*]

THE ROUGH — [*As they are going out.*] This silly bloke'll 'ave the s'prise of 'is life when 'e wakes up on board of 'er. [*They laugh. The door closes behind them.* FREDA *moves quickly for the door on the left but* JOE *gets in her way and stops her.*]

JOE — [*Threateningly.*] Guv us what yer took!

FREDA — Took? I guv yer all 'e 'ad.

JOE — Yer a liar! I seen yer a-playin' yer sneakin' tricks, but yer can't fool Joe. I'm too old a 'and. [*Furiously.*] Guv it to me, yer bloody cow! [*He grabs her by the arm.*]

FREDA — Lemme alone! I ain't got no —

JOE — [*Hits her viciously on the side of the jaw. She crumples up on the floor.*] That'll learn yer! [*He stoops down and fumbles in her bosom and pulls out the banknote, which he stuffs into his pocket with a grunt of satisfaction.* KATE *opens the door on the left and looks in — then rushes to* FREDA *and lifts her head up in her arms.*]

KATE — [*Gently.*] Pore dearie! [*Looking at* JOE *angrily.*] Been 'ittin' 'er agen, 'ave yer, yer cowardly swine!

JOE — Yus; an' I'll 'it you, too, if yer don't keep yer marf shut. Tike 'er aht of 'ere! [KATE *carries* FREDA *into the next room.* JOE *goes behind the bar. A moment later the outer door is opened and* DRISCOLL *and* COCKY *come in.*]

DRISCOLL — Come on, Ollie. [*He suddenly sees that* OLSON *is not there, and turns to* JOE.] Where is ut he's gone to?

JOE — [*With a meaning wink.*] 'E an' Freda went aht t'gether 'bout five minutes past. 'E's fair gone on 'er, 'e is.

DRISCOLL — [*With a grin.*] Oho, so that's ut, is ut? Who'd think Ollie'd be sich a divil wid the wimin? 'Tis lucky he's sober or she'd have him stripped to his last ha'penny. [*Turning to* COCKY, *who is blinking sleepily.*] What'll ye have, ye little scut? [*To* JOE.] Give me whiskey, *Irish* whiskey!

[*The Curtain Falls*]

In the Zone

A PLAY IN ONE ACT

CHARACTERS

SMITTY
DAVIS
SWANSON
SCOTTY
IVAN   } *Seamen on the British tramp steamer*
PAUL   Glencairn
JACK
DRISCOLL
COCKY

SCENE — *The seamen's forecastle. On the right above the bunks three or four portholes covered with black cloth can be seen. On the floor near the doorway is a pail with a tin dipper. A lantern in the middle of the floor, turned down very low, throws a dim light around the place. Five men,* SCOTTY, IVAN, SWANSON, SMITTY *and* PAUL, *are in their bunks apparently asleep. It is about ten minutes of twelve on a night in the fall of the year 1915.*

SMITTY *turns slowly in his bunk and, leaning out over the side, looks from one to another of the men as if to assure himself that they are asleep. Then he climbs carefully out of his bunk and stands in the middle of the forecastle fully dressed, but in his stocking feet, glancing around him suspiciously. Reassured, he leans down and cautiously pulls out a suit-case from under the bunks in front of him.*

Just at this moment DAVIS *appears in the doorway, carrying a large steaming coffee-pot in his hand. He stops short when he sees* SMITTY. *A puzzled expression comes over his face, followed by one of suspicion, and he retreats farther back in the alleyway, where he can watch* SMITTY *without being seen.*

All the latter's movements indicate a fear of discovery. He takes out a small bunch of keys and unlocks the suit-case, making a slight noise as he does so. SCOTTY *wakes up and peers at him over the side of the bunk.* SMITTY *opens the suit-case and takes out a small black tin box, carefully places this under his mattress, shoves the suit-case back under the bunk, climbs into his bunk again, closes his eyes and begins to snore loudly.*

DAVIS *enters the forecastle, places the coffee-pot beside the lantern, and goes from one to the other of the sleepers and shakes them vigorously, saying to each in a low voice:* Near eight bells, Scotty. Arise and shine, Swanson. Eight bells, Ivan. SMITTY *yawns loudly with a great pretense of having been dead asleep. All of the rest of the men tumble out of their bunks, stretching and gaping, and commence to pull on their shoes. They go one by one to the cupboard near the open door, take out their cups and spoons, and sit down together on the benches. The coffee-pot is passed around. They munch their biscuits and sip their coffee in dull silence.*

DAVIS — [*Suddenly jumping to his feet — nervously.*] Where's that air comin' from? [*All are startled and look at him wonderingly.*]

SWANSON — [*A squat, surly-faced Swede — grumpily.*] What air? I don't feel nothing.

DAVIS — [*Excitedly.*] I kin feel it — a draft. [*He stands on the bench and looks around — suddenly exploding.*] Damn fool square-head! [*He leans over the upper bunk in which* PAUL *is sleeping and slams the porthole shut.*] I got a good notion to report him. Serve him bloody well right! What's the use o' blindin' the ports when that thick-head goes an' leaves 'em open?

SWANSON — [*Yawning — too sleepy to be aroused by anything — carelessly.*] Dey don't see what little light go out yust one port.

SCOTTY — [*Protestingly.*] Dinna be a loon, Swanson! D'ye no ken the dangerr o' showin' a licht wi' a pack o' submarrines lyin' aboot?

IVAN — [*Shaking his shaggy ox-like head in an emphatic affirmative.*] Dot's right, Scotty. I don' li-ike blow up, no, by devil!

SMITTY — [*His manner slightly contemptuous.*] I don't think there's much danger of meeting any of their submarines, not until we get into the War Zone, at any rate.

DAVIS — [*He and* SCOTTY *look at* SMITTY *suspiciously — harshly.*] You don't, eh? [*He lowers his voice and speaks slowly.*] Well, we're in the war zone right this minit if you wants to know. [*The effect of this speech is instantaneous. All sit bolt upright on their benches and stare at Davis.*]

SMITTY — How do you know, Davis?

DAVIS — [*Angrily.*] 'Cos Drisc heard the First send the Third below to wake the skipper when we fetched the zone—bout five bells, it was. Now whata y' got to say?

SMITTY—[*Conciliatingly.*] Oh, I wasn't doubting your word, Davis; but you know they're not pasting up bulletins to let the crew know when the zone is reached—especially on ammunition ships like this.

IVAN—[*Decidedly.*] I don't li-ike dees voyage. Next time I ship on windjammer Boston to River Plate, load with wood only so it float, by golly!

SWANSON—[*Fretfully.*] I hope British navy blow 'em to hell, those submarines, py damn!

SCOTTY—[*Looking at* SMITTY, *who is staring at the doorway in a dream, his chin on his hands. Meaningly.*] It is no the submarrines only we've to fear, I'm thinkin'.

DAVIS—[*Assenting eagerly.*] That's no lie, Scotty.

SWANSON—You mean the mines?

SCOTTY—I wasna thinkin' o' mines eitherr.

DAVIS—There's many a good ship blown up and at the bottom of the sea, what never hit no mine or torpedo.

SCOTTY—Did ye neverr read of the Gerrman spies and the dirrty work they're doin' all the war? [*He and* DAVIS *both glance at* SMITTY, *who is deep in thought and is not listening to the conversation.*]

DAVIS—An' the clever way they fool you!

SWANSON—Sure; I read it in paper many time.

DAVIS—Well—[*He is about to speak but hesitates and finishes lamely.*] you got to watch out, that's all I says.

IVAN—[*Drinking the last of his coffee and slamming his fist on the bench explosively.*] I tell you dis rotten coffee give me belly-ache, yes! [*They all look at him in amused disgust.*]

SCOTTY—[*Sardonically.*] Dinna fret about it, Ivan. If we blow up ye'll no be mindin' the pain in your middle. [JACK *enters. He is a young American with a tough, good-natured face. He wears dungarees and a heavy jersey.*]

JACK—Eight bells, fellers.

IVAN—[*Stupidly.*] I don' hear bell ring.

JACK—No, and yuh won't hear any ring, yuh boob—[*Lowering his voice unconsciously.*] now we're in the war zone.

SWANSON—[*Anxiously.*] Is the boats all ready?

JACK—Sure; we can lower 'em in a second.

DAVIS—A lot o' good the boats'll do, with us loaded deep with all kinds o' dynamite and stuff the like o' that! If a torpedo hits this hooker we'll all be in hell b'fore you could wink your eye.

JACK—They ain't goin' to hit us, see? That's my dope. Whose wheel is it?

IVAN—[*Sullenly.*] My wheel. [*He lumbers out.*]

JACK—And whose lookout?

SWANSON—Mine, I tink. [*He follows* IVAN.]

JACK—[*Scornfully.*] A hell of a lot of use keepin' a lookout! We couldn't run away or fight if we wanted to. [*To* SCOTTY *and* SMITTY.] Better look up the bo'sun or the Fourth, you two, and let 'em see you're awake. [SCOTTY *goes to the doorway and turns to wait for* SMITTY, *who is still in the same position, head on hands, seemingly unconscious of everything.* JACK *slaps him roughly on the shoulder and he comes to with a start.*] Aft and report, Duke! What's the matter with yuh—in a dope dream? [SMITTY *goes out after* SCOTTY *without answering.* JACK *looks after him with a frown.*] He's a queer guy. I can't figger him out.

DAVIS—Nor no one else. [*Lowering his voice—meaningly.*] An' he's liable to turn out queerer than any of us think if we ain't careful.

JACK—[*Suspiciously.*] What d'yuh mean? [*They are interrupted by the entrance of* DRISCOLL *and* COCKY.]

COCKY—[*Protestingly.*] Blimey if I don't fink I'll put in this 'ere watch ahtside on deck. [*He and* DRISCOLL *go over and get their cups.*] I down't want to be caught in this 'ole if they 'its us. [*He pours out coffee.*]

DRISCOLL—[*Pouring his.*] Divil a bit ut wud matther where ye arre. Ye'd be blown to smithereens b'fore ye cud say your name. [*He sits down, overturning as he does so the untouched cup of coffee which* SMITTY *had forgotten and left on the bench. They all jump nervously as the tin cup hits the floor with a bang.* DRISCOLL *flies into an unreasoning rage.*] Who's the dirty scut left this cup where a man 'ud sit on ut?

DAVIS—It's Smitty's.

DRISCOLL—[*Kicking the cup across the forecastle.*] Does he think he's too much av a bloody gentleman to put his own away loike the rist av us? If he does I'm the bye'll beat that noshun out av his head.

COCKY—Be the airs 'e puts on you'd think 'e was the Prince of Wales. Wot's 'e doin' on a ship, I arsks yer? 'E ain't now good as a sailor, is 'e?— dawdlin' abaht on deck like a chicken wiv 'is 'ead cut orf!

JACK — [*Good-naturedly.*] Aw, the Duke's all right. S'posin' he did ferget his cup — what's the dif? [*He picks up the cup and puts it away — with a grin.*] This war zone stuff's got yer goat, Drisc — and yours too, Cocky — and I ain't cheerin' much fur it myself, neither.

COCKY — [*With a sigh.*] Blimey, it ain't no bleedin' joke, yer first trip, to know as there's a ship full of shells li'ble to go orf in under your bloomin' feet, as you might say, if we gets 'it be a torpedo or mine. [*With sudden savagery.*] Calls theyselves 'uman bein's, too! Blarsted 'Uns!

DRISCOLL — [*Gloomily.*] 'Tis me last trip in the bloody zone, God help me. The divil take their twenty-foive percent bonus — and be drowned like a rat in a trap in the bargain, maybe.

DAVIS — Wouldn't be so bad if she wasn't carryin' ammunition. Them's the kind the subs is layin' for.

DRISCOLL — [*Irritably.*] Fur the love av hivin, don't be talkin' about ut. I'm sick wid thinkin' and jumpin' at iviry bit av a noise. [*There is a pause during which they all stare gloomily at the floor.*]

JACK — Hey, Davis, what was you sayin' about Smitty when they come in?

DAVIS — [*With a great air of mystery.*] I'll tell you in a minit. I want to wait an' see if he's comin' back. [*Impressively.*] You won't be callin' him all right when you hears what I seen with my own eyes. [*He adds with an air of satisfaction.*] An' you won't be feelin' no safer, neither. [*They all look at him with puzzled glances full of a vague apprehension.*]

DRISCOLL — God blarst ut! [*He fills his pipe and lights it. The others, with an air of remembering something they had forgotten, do the same. SCOTTY enters.*]

SCOTTY — [*In awed tones.*] Mon, but it's clear outside the nicht! Like day.

DAVIS — [*In low tones.*] Where's Smitty, Scotty?

SCOTTY — Out on the hatch starin' at the moon like a mon half-daft.

DAVIS — Kin you see him from the doorway?

SCOTTY — [*Goes to doorway and carefully peeks out.*] Aye; he's still there.

DAVIS — Keep your eyes on him for a moment. I've got something I wants to tell the boys and I don't want him walkin' in in the middle of it. Give a shout if he starts this way.

SCOTTY — [*With suppressed excitement.*] Aye, I'll watch him. And I've somethin' myself to tell aboot his Lordship.

DRISCOLL — [*Impatiently.*] Out wid ut! You're talkin' more than a pair av auld women wud be standin' in the road, and gittin' no further along.

DAVIS — Listen! You 'member when I went to git the coffee, Jack?

JACK — Sure, I do.

DAVIS — Well, I brings it down here same as usual and got as far as the door there when I sees him.

JACK — Smitty?

DAVIS — Yes, Smitty! He was standin' in the middle of the fo'c's'tle there [*Pointing.*] lookin' around sneakin'-like at Ivan and Swanson and the rest's if he wants to make certain they're asleep. [*He pauses significantly, looking from one to the other of his listeners.* SCOTTY *is nervously dividing his attention between* SMITTY *on the hatch outside and* DAVIS' *story, fairly bursting to break in with his own revelations.*]

JACK — [*Impatiently.*] What of it?

DAVIS — Listen! He was standin' right there — [*Pointing again.*] in his stockin' feet — no shoes on, mind, so he wouldn't make no noise!

JACK — [*Spitting disgustedly.*] Aw!

DAVIS — [*Not heeding the interruption.*] I seen right away somethin' on the queer was up so I slides back into the alleyway where I kin see him but he can't see me. After he makes sure they're all asleep he goes in under the bunks there — bein' careful not to raise a noise, mind! — an' takes out his bag there. [*By this time every one,* JACK *included, is listening breathlessly to his story.*] Then he fishes in his pocket an' takes out a bunch o' keys an' kneels down beside the bag an' opens it.

SCOTTY — [*Unable to keep silent longer.*] Mon, didn't I see him do that same thing wi' these two eyes. 'Twas just that moment I woke and spied him.

DAVIS — [*Surprised, and a bit nettled to have to share his story with any one.*] Oh, you seen him too, eh? [*To the others.*] Then Scotty kin tell you if I'm lyin' or not.

DRISCOLL — An' what did he do whin he'd the bag opened?

DAVIS — He bends down and reaches out his hand sort o' scared-like, like it was somethin' dang'rous he was after, an' feels round in under his duds — hidden in under his duds an' wrapped up in 'em, it was — an' he brings out a black iron box!

COCKY — [*Looking around him with a frightened glance.*] Gawd blimey! [*The others likewise betray their uneasiness, shuffling their feet nervously.*]

DAVIS — Ain't that right, Scotty?

SCOTTY — Right as rain, I'm tellin' ye'!

DAVIS — [*To the others with an air of satisfaction.*] There you are! [*Lowering his voice.*] An' then what d'you suppose he did? Sneaks to his bunk an' slips the black box in under his mattress — in under his mattress, mind! —

JACK — And it's there now?

DAVIS — Course it is! [JACK *starts toward* SMITTY'S *bunk.* DRISCOLL *grabs him by the arm.*]

DRISCOLL — Don't be touchin' ut, Jack!

JACK — Yuh needn't worry. I ain't goin' to touch it. [*He pulls up* SMITTY'S *mattress and looks down. The others stare at him, holding their breaths. He turns to them, trying hard to assume a careless tone.*] It's there, aw right.

COCKY — [*Miserably upset.*] I'm gointer 'op it aht on deck. [*He gets up but* DRISCOLL *pulls him down again.* COCKY *protests.*] It fair guvs me the trembles sittin' still in 'ere.

DRISCOLL — [*Scornfully.*] Are ye frightened, ye toad? 'Tis a hell av a thing fur grown men to be shiverin' loike childer at a bit av a black box. [*Scratching his head in uneasy perplexity.*] Still, ut's damn queer, the looks av ut.

DAVIS — [*Sarcastically.*] A bit of a black box, eh? How big d'you think them — [*He hesitates*] — things has to be — big as this fo'c's'tle?

JACK — [*In a voice meant to be reassuring.*] Aw, hell! I'll bet it ain't nothin' but some coin he's saved he's got locked up in there.

DAVIS — [*Scornfully.*] That's likely, ain't it? Then why does he act so s'picious? He's been on ship near two year, ain't he? He knows damn well there ain't no thiefs in this fo'c's'tle, don't he? An' you know 's well 's I do he didn't have no money when he came on board an' he ain't saved none since. Don't you? [JACK *doesn't answer.*] Listen! D'you know what he done after he put that thing in under his mattress? — an' Scotty'll tell you if I ain't speakin' truth. He looks round to see if any one's woke up —

SCOTTY — I clapped my eyes shut when he turned round.

DAVIS — An' then he crawls into his bunk an' shuts his eyes, an' starts in *snorin', pretendin'* he was asleep, mind!

SCOTTY—Aye, I could hear him.

DAVIS—An' when I goes to call him I don't even shake him. I just says, "Eight bells, Smitty," in a'most a whisper-like, an' up he gets yawnin' an' stretchin' fit to kill hisself 's if he'd been dead asleep.

COCKY—Gawd blimey!

DRISCOLL—[*Shaking his head.*] Ut looks bad, divil a doubt av ut.

DAVIS—[*Excitedly.*] An' now I come to think of it, there's the port-hole. How'd it come to git open, tell me that? I know'd well Paul never opened it. Ain't he grumblin' about bein' cold all the time?

SCOTTY—The mon that opened it meant no good to this ship, whoever he was.

JACK—[*Sourly.*] What porthole? What're yuh talkin' about?

DAVIS—[*Pointing over* PAUL'S *bunk.*] There. It was open when I come in. I felt the cold air on my neck an' shut it. It would'a been clear's a lighthouse to any sub that was watchin'—an' we s'posed to have all the ports blinded! Who'd do a dirty trick like that? It wasn't none of us, nor Scotty here, nor Swanson, nor Ivan. Who would it be, then?

COCKY—[*Angrily.*] Must'a been 'is bloody Lordship.

DAVIS—For all's we know he might'a been signallin' with it. They does it like that by winkin' a light. Ain't you read how they gets caught doin' it in London an' on the coast?

COCKY—[*Firmly convinced now.*] An' wots 'e doin' aht alone on the 'atch—keepin' 'isself clear of us like 'e was afraid?

DRISCOLL—Kape your eye on him, Scotty.

SCOTTY—There's no a move oot o' him.

JACK—[*In irritated perplexity.*] But, hell, ain't he an Englishman? What'd he wanta——

DAVIS—English? How d'we know he's English? Cos he talks it? That ain't no proof. Ain't you read in the papers how all them German spies they been catchin' in England has been livin' there for ten, often as not twenty years, an' talks English as good's any one? An' look here, ain't you noticed he don't talk natural? He talks it too damn good, that's what I mean. He don't talk exactly like a toff, does he, Cocky?

COCKY—Not like any toff as I ever met up wiv.

DAVIS—No; an' he don't talk it like us, that's certain. An' he don't look English. An' what d'we know about him when you come to look at it? Nothin'! He ain't ever said where he comes from or why. All we knows is he ships on here in London 'bout a year b'fore the war starts, as an A. B. — stole his papers most lik'ly — when he don't know how to box the compass, hardly. Ain't that queer in itself? An' was he ever open with us like a good shipmate? No; he's always had that sly air about him 's if he was hidin' somethin'.

DRISCOLL — [*Slapping his thigh — angrily.*] Divil take me if I don't think ye have the truth av ut, Davis.

COCKY — [*Scornfully.*] Lettin' on be 'is silly airs, and all, 'e's the son of a blarsted earl or somethink!

DAVIS — An' the name he calls hisself — Smith! I'd risk a quid of my next pay day that his real name is Schmidt, if the truth was known.

JACK — [*Evidently fighting against his own conviction.*] Aw, say, you guys give me a pain! What'd they want puttin' a spy on this old tub for?

DAVIS — [*Shaking his head sagely.*] They're deep ones, an' there's a lot o' things a sailor'll see in the ports he puts in ought to be useful to 'em. An' if he kin signal to 'em an' they blows us up it's one ship less, ain't it? [*Lowering his voice and indicating* SMITTY'S *bunk.*] Or if he blows us up hisself.

SCOTTY — [*In alarmed tones.*] Hush, mon! Here he comes! [SCOTTY *hurries over to a bench and sits down. A thick silence settles over the forecastle. The men look from one to another with uneasy glances.* SMITTY *enters and sits down beside his bunk. He is seemingly unaware of the dark glances of suspicion directed at him from all sides. He slides his hand back stealthily over his mattress and his fingers move, evidently feeling to make sure the box is still there. The others follow this movement carefully with quick looks out of the corners of their eyes. Their attitudes grow tense as if they were about to spring at him. Satisfied the box is safe,* SMITTY *draws his hand away slowly and utters a sigh of relief.*]

SMITTY — [*In a casual tone which to them sounds sinister.*] It's a good light night for the subs if there's any about. [*For a moment he sits staring in front of him. Finally he seems to sense the hostile atmosphere of the forecastle and looks from one to the other of the men in surprise. All of them avoid his eyes. He sighs with a puzzled expression and gets up and walks out of the doorway. There is silence for a moment after his departure and then a storm of excited talk breaks loose.*]

DAVIS — Did you see him feelin' if it was there?

COCKY — 'E ain't arf a sly one wiv 'is talk of submarines, Gawd blind 'im!

SCOTTY — Did ye see the sneakin' looks he gave us?

DRISCOLL — If ivir I saw black shame on a man's face 'twas on his whin he sat there!

JACK — [_Thoroughly convinced at last._] He looked bad to me. He's a crook, aw right.

DAVIS — [_Excitedly._] What'll we do? We gotter do somethin' quick or —— [_He is interrupted by the sound of something hitting against the port side of the forecastle with a dull, heavy thud. The men start to their feet in wild-eyed terror and turn as if they were going to rush for the deck. They stand that way for a strained moment, scarcely breathing and listening intently._]

JACK — [_With a sickly smile._] Hell! It's on'y a piece of driftwood or a floatin' log. [_He sits down again._]

DAVIS — [_Sarcastically._] Or a mine that didn't go off — that time — or a piece o' wreckage from some ship they've sent to Davy Jones.

COCKY — [_Mopping his brow with a trembling hand._] Blimey! [_He sinks back weakly on a bench._]

DRISCOLL — [_Furiously._] God blarst ut! No man at all cud be puttin' up wid the loike av this — an' I'm not wan to be fearin' anything or any man in the worrld'll stand up to me face to face; but this divil's trickery in the darrk —— [_He starts for_ SMITTY'S _bunk._] I'll throw ut out wan av the portholes an' be done wid ut. [_He reaches toward the mattress._]

SCOTTY — [_Grabbing his arm — wildly._] Arre ye daft, mon?

DAVIS — Don't monkey with it, Drisc. I knows what to do. Bring the bucket o' water here, Jack, will you? [JACK _gets it and brings it over to_ DAVIS.] An' you, Scotty, see if he's back on the hatch.

SCOTTY — [_Cautiously peering out._] Aye, he's sittin' there the noo.

DAVIS — Sing out if he makes a move. Lift up the mattress, Drisc — careful now! [DRISCOLL _does so with infinite caution._] Take it out, Jack — careful — don't shake it now, for Christ's sake! Here — put it in the water — easy! There, that's fixed it! [_They all sit down with great sighs of relief._] The water'll git in and spoil it.

DRISCOLL — [_Slapping_ DAVIS _on the back._] Good wurrk for ye, Davis, ye scut! [_He spits on his hands aggressively._] An' now what's to be done wid that black-hearted thraitor?

COCKY—[*Belligerently.*] Guv 'im a shove in the marf and 'eave 'im over the side!

DAVIS—An' serve him right!

JACK—Aw, say, give him a chance. Yuh can't prove nothin' till yuh find out what's in there.

DRISCOLL—[*Heatedly.*] Is ut more proof ye'd be needin' afther what we've seen an' heard? Then listen to me—an' ut's Driscoll talkin'—if there's divilmint in that box an' we see plain 'twas his plan to murrdher his own shipmates that have served him fair—— [*He raises his fist.*] I'll choke his rotten hearrt out wid me own hands, an' over the side wid him, and one man missin' in the mornin'.

DAVIS—An' no one the wiser. He's the balmy kind what commits suicide.

COCKY—They 'angs spies ashore.

JACK—[*Resentfully.*] If he's done what yuh think I'll croak him myself. Is that good enough for yuh?

DRISCOLL—[*Looking down at the box.*] How'll we be openin' this, I wonder?

SCOTTY—[*From the doorway—warningly.*] He's standin' up.

DAVIS—We'll take his keys away from him when he comes in. Quick, Drisc! You an' Jack get beside the door and grab him. [*They get on either side of the door. DAVIS snatches a small coil of rope from one of the upper bunks.*] This'll do for me an' Scotty to tie him.

SCOTTY—He's turrnin' this way—he's comin'! [*He moves away from door.*]

DAVIS—Stand by to lend a hand, Cocky.

COCKY—Righto. [*As SMITTY enters the forecastle he is seized roughly from both sides and his arms pinned behind him. At first he struggles fiercely, but seeing the uselessness of this, he finally stands calmly and allows DAVIS and SCOTTY to tie up his arms.*]

SMITTY—[*When they have finished—with cold contempt.*] If this is your idea of a joke I'll have to confess it's a bit too thick for me to enjoy.

COCKY—[*Angrily.*] Shut yer marf, 'ear!

DRISCOLL—[*Roughly.*] Ye'll find ut's no joke, me bucko, b'fore we're done wid you. [*To SCOTTY.*] Kape your eye peeled, Scotty, and sing out if any one's comin'. [*SCOTTY resumes his post at the door.*]

SMITTY — [*With the same icy contempt.*] If you'd be good enough to explain ——

DRISCOLL — [*Furiously.*] Explain, is ut? 'Tis you'll do the explainin' — an' damn quick, or we'll know the reason why. [*To* JACK *and* DAVIS.] Bring him here, now. [*They push* SMITTY *over to the bucket.*] Look here, ye murrdherin' swab. D'you see ut? [SMITTY *looks down with an expression of amazement which rapidly changes to one of anguish.*]

DAVIS — [*With a sneer.*] Look at him! S'prised, ain't you? If you wants to try your dirty spyin' tricks on us you've gotter git up earlier in the mornin'.

COCKY — Thorght yer weren't 'arf a fox, didn't yer?

SMITTY — [*Trying to restrain his growing rage.*] What — what do you mean? That's only — How dare — What are you doing with my private belongings?

COCKY — [*Sarcastically.*] Ho yus! Private b'longings!

DRISCOLL — [*Shouting.*] What is ut, ye swine? Will you tell us to our faces? What's in ut?

SMITTY — [*Biting his lips — holding himself in check with a great effort.*] Nothing but —— That's my business. You'll please attend to your own.

DRISCOLL — Oho, ut is, is ut? [*Shaking his fist in* SMITTY'S *face.*] Talk aisy now if ye know what's best for you. Your business, indade! Then we'll be makin' ut ours, I'm thinkin'. [*To* JACK *and* DAVIS.] Take his keys away from him an' we'll see if there's one'll open ut, maybe. [*They start in searching* SMITTY, *who tries to resist and kicks out at the bucket.* DRISCOLL *leaps forward and helps them push him away.*] Try to kick ut over, wud ye? Did ye see him then? Tryin' to murrdher us all, the scut! Take that pail out av his way, Cocky. [SMITTY *struggles with all of his strength and keeps them busy for a few seconds. As* COCKY *grabs the pail* SMITTY *makes a final effort and, lunging forward, kicks again at the bucket but only succeeds in hitting* COCKY *on the shin.* COCKY *immediately sets down the pail with a bang and, clutching his knee in both hands, starts hopping around the forecastle, groaning and swearing.*]

COCKY — Ooow! Gawd strike me pink! Kicked me, 'e did! Bloody, bleedin', rotten Dutch 'og! [*Approaching* SMITTY, *who has given up the fight and is pushed back against the wall near the doorway with* JACK *and* DAVIS *holding him on either side — wrathfully, at the top of his lungs.*]

Kick me, will yer? I'll show yer what for, yer bleedin' sneak! [*He draws back his fist.* DRISCOLL *pushes him to one side.*]

DRISCOLL — Shut your mouth! D'you want to wake the whole ship? [COCKY *grumbles and retires to a bench, nursing his sore shin.*]

JACK — [*Taking a small bunch of keys from* SMITTY'S *pocket.*] Here yuh are, Drisc.

DRISCOLL — [*Taking them.*] We'll soon be knowin'. [*He takes the pail and sits down, placing it on the floor between his feet.* SMITTY *again tries to break loose but he is too tired and is easily held back against the wall.*]

SMITTY — [*Breathing heavily and very pale.*] Cowards!

JACK — [*With a growl.*] Nix on the rough talk, see! That don't git yuh nothin'.

DRISCOLL — [*Looking at the lock on the box in the water and then scrutinizing the keys in his hand.*] This'll be ut, I'm thinkin'. [*He selects one and gingerly reaches his hand in the water.*]

SMITTY — [*His face grown livid — chokingly.*] Don't you open that box, Driscoll. If you do, so help me God, I'll kill you if I have to hang for it.

DRISCOLL — [*Pausing — his hand in the water.*] Whin I open this box I'll not be the wan to be kilt, me sonny bye! I'm no dirty spy.

SMITTY — [*His voice trembling with rage. His eyes are fixed on* DRISCOLL'S *hand.*] Spy? What are you talking about? I only put that box there so I could get it quick in case we were torpedoed. Are you all mad? Do you think I'm — [*Chokingly.*] You stupid curs! You cowardly dolts! [DAVIS *claps his hand over* SMITTY'S *mouth.*]

DAVIS — That'll be enough from you! [DRISCOLL *takes the dripping box from the water and starts to fit in the key.* SMITTY *springs forward furiously, almost escaping from their grasp, and drags them after him halfway across the forecastle.*]

DRISCOLL — Hold him, ye divils! [*He puts the box back in the water and jumps to their aid.* COCKY *hovers on the outskirts of the battle, mindful of the kick he received.*]

SMITTY — [*Raging.*] Cowards! Damn you! Rotten curs! [*He is thrown to the floor and held there.*] Cowards! Cowards!

DRISCOLL — I'll shut your dirty mouth for you. [*He goes to his bunk and pulls out a big wad of waste and comes back to* SMITTY.]

SMITTY — Cowards! Cowards!

DRISCOLL — [*With no gentle hand slaps the waste over* SMITTY'S *mouth.*] That'll teach you to be misnamin' a man, ye sneak. Have ye a handkerchief, Jack? [JACK *hands him one and he ties it tightly around* SMITTY'S *head over the waste.*] That'll fix your gab. Stand him up, now, and tie his feet, too, so he'll not be movin'. [*They do so and leave him with his back against the wall near* SCOTTY. *Then they all sit down beside* DRISCOLL, *who again lifts the box out of the water and sets it carefully on his knees. He picks out the key, then hesitates, looking from one to the other uncertainly.*] We'd best be takin' this to the skipper, d'you think, maybe?

JACK — [*Irritably.*] To hell with the Old Man. This is our game and we c'n play it without no help.

COCKY — Now bleedin' horficers, I says!

DAVIS — They'd only be takin' all the credit and makin' heroes of theyselves.

DRISCOLL — [*Boldly.*] Here goes, thin! [*He slowly turns the key in the lock. The others instinctively turn away. He carefully pushes the cover back on its hinges and looks at what he sees inside with an expression of puzzled astonishment. The others crowd up close. Even* SCOTTY *leaves his post to take a look.*] What is ut, Davis?

DAVIS — [*Mystified.*] Looks funny, don't it? Somethin' square tied up in a rubber bag. Maybe it's dynamite — or somethin' — you can't never tell.

JACK — Aw, it ain't got no works so it ain't no bomb, I'll bet.

DAVIS — [*Dubiously.*] They makes them all kinds, they do.

JACK — Open it up, Drisc.

DAVIS — Careful now! [DRISCOLL *takes a black rubber bag resembling a large tobacco pouch from the box and unties the string which is wound tightly around the top. He opens it and takes out a small packet of letters also tied up with string. He turns these over in his hands and looks at the others questioningly.*]

JACK — [*With a broad grin.*] On'y letters! [*Slapping* DAVIS *on the back.*] Yuh're a hell of a Sherlock Holmes, ain't yuh? Letters from his best girl too, I'll bet. Let's turn the Duke loose, what d'yuh say? [*He starts to get up.*]

DAVIS — [*Fixing him with a withering look.*] Don't be so damn smart, Jack. Letters, you says, 's if there never was no harm in 'em. How d'you s'pose spies gets their orders and sends back what they finds out if it ain't by letters and such things? There's many a letter is worser'n any bomb.

COCKY—Righto! They ain't as innercent as they looks, I'll take me oath, when you read 'em. [*Pointing at* SMITTY.] Not 'is Lordship's letters; not be no means!

JACK—[*Sitting down again.*] Well, read 'em and find out. [DRISCOLL *commences untying the packet. There is a muffled groan of rage and protest from* SMITTY.]

DAVIS—[*Triumphantly.*] There! Listen to him! Look at him tryin' to git loose! Ain't that proof enough? He knows well we're findin' him out. Listen to me! Love letters, you says, Jack, 's if they couldn't harm nothin'. Listen! I was readin' in some magazine in New York on'y two weeks back how some German spy in Paris was writin' love letters to some woman spy in Switzerland who sent 'em on to Berlin, Germany. To read 'em you wouldn't s'pect nothin'—just mush and all. [*Impressively.*] But they had a way o' doin' it—a damn sneakin' way. They had a piece o' plain paper with pieces cut out of it an' when they puts it on top o' the letter they sees on'y the words what tells them what they wants to know. An' the Frenchies gets beat in a fight all on account o' that letter.

COCKY—[*Awed.*] Gawd blimey! They ain't 'arf smart bleeders!

DAVIS—[*Seeing his audience is again all with him.*] An' even if these letters of his do sound all right they may have what they calls a code. You can't never tell. [*To* DRISCOLL, *who has finished untying the packet.*] Read one of 'em, Drisc. My eyes is weak.

DRISCOLL—[*Takes the first one out of its envelope and bends down to the lantern with it. He turns up the wick to give him a better light.*] I'm no hand to be readin' but I'll try ut. [*Again there is a muffled groan from* SMITTY *as he strains at his bonds.*]

DAVIS—[*Gloatingly.*] Listen to him! He knows. Go ahead, Drisc!

DRISCOLL—[*His brow furrowed with concentration.*] Ut begins: Dearest Man—— [*His eyes travel down the page.*] An' thin there's a lot av blarney tellin' him how much she misses him now she's gone away to singin' school—an' how she hopes he'll settle down to rale worrk an' not be skylarkin' around now that she's away loike he used to before she met up wid him—and ut ends: "I love you betther than anythin' in the worrld. You know that, don't you, dear? But b'fore I can agree to live out my life wid you, you must prove to me that the black shadow—I won't menshun uts hateful name but you know what I mean—which might wreck both our lives, does not exist for you. You can do that, can't you, dear? Don't you see you must for my sake?" [*He pauses for a moment—*

then adds gruffly.] Uts signed: "Edith." [*At the sound of the name* SMITTY, *who has stood tensely with his eyes shut as if he were undergoing torture during the reading, makes a muffled sound like a sob and half turns his face to the wall.*]

JACK — [*Sympathetically.*] Hell! What's the use of readin' that stuff even if —

DAVIS — [*Interrupting him sharply.*] Wait! Where's that letter from, Drisc?

DRISCOLL — There's no address on the top av ut.

DAVIS — [*Meaningly.*] What'd I tell you? Look at the postmark, Drisc, — on the envelope.

DRISCOLL — The name that's written is Sidney Davidson, wan hundred an' —

DAVIS — Never mind that. O' course it's a false name. Look at the postmark.

DRISCOLL — There's a furrin stamp on ut by the looks av ut. The mark's blurred so it's hard to read. [*He spells it out laboriously.*] B-e-r — the nixt is an l, I think — i — an' an n.

DAVIS — [*Excitedly.*] Berlin! What did I tell you? I knew them letters was from Germany.

COCKY — [*Shaking his fist in* SMITTY'S *direction.*] Rotten 'ound! [*The others look at* SMITTY *as if this last fact had utterly condemned him in their eyes.*]

DAVIS — Give me the letter, Drisc. Maybe I kin make somethin' out of it. [DRISCOLL *hands the letter to him.*] You go through the others, Drisc, and sing out if you sees anythin' queer. [*He bends over the first letter as if he were determined to figure out its secret meaning.* JACK, COCKY *and* SCOTTY *look over his shoulder with eager curiosity.* DRISCOLL *takes out some of the other letters, running his eyes quickly down the pages. He looks curiously over at* SMITTY *from time to time, and sighs frequently with a puzzled frown.*]

DAVIS — [*Disappointedly.*] I gotter give it up. It's too deep for me, but we'll turn 'em over to the perlice when we docks at Liverpool to look through. This one I got was written a year before the war started, anyway. Find anythin' in yours, Drisc?

DRISCOLL — They're all the same as the first — lovin' blarney, an' how her singin' is doin', and the great things the Dutch teacher says about her voice, an' how glad she is that her Sidney bye is workin' harrd an' makin' a man av himself for her sake. [SMITTY *turns his face completely to the wall.*]

DAVIS—[*Disgustedly.*] If we on'y had the code!

DRISCOLL—[*Taking up the bottom letter.*] Hullo! Here's wan addressed to this ship—S. S. *Glencairn,* ut says—whin we was in Cape Town sivin months ago—— [*Looking at the postmark.*] Ut's from London.

DAVIS—[*Eagerly.*] Read it! [*There is another choking groan from* SMITTY.]

DRISCOLL—[*Reads slowly—his voice becomes lower and lower as he goes on.*] Ut begins wid simply the name Sidney Davidson—no dearest or sweetheart to this wan. "Ut is only from your chance meetin' wid Harry—whin you were drunk—that I happen to know where to reach you. So you have run away to sea loike the coward you are because you knew I had found out the truth—the truth you have covered over with your mean little lies all the time I was away in Berlin and blindly trusted you. Very well, you have chosen. You have shown that your drunkenness means more to you than any love or faith av mine. I am sorry—for I loved you, Sidney Davidson—but this is the end. I lave you—the mem'ries; an' if ut is any satisfaction to you I lave you the real-i-zation that you have wrecked my loife as you have wrecked your own. My one remainin' hope is that nivir in God's worrld will I ivir see your face again. Good-by. Edith." [*As he finishes there is a deep silence, broken only by* SMITTY'S *muffled sobbing. The men cannot look at each other.* DRISCOLL *holds the rubber bag limply in his hand and some small white object falls out of it and drops noiselessly on the floor. Mechanically* DRISCOLL *leans over and picks it up, and looks at it wonderingly.*]

DAVIS—[*In a dull voice.*] What's that?

DRISCOLL—[*Slowly.*] A bit av a dried-up flower,—a rose, maybe. [*He drops it into the bag and gathers up the letters and puts them back. He replaces the bag in the box, and locks it and puts it back under* SMITTY'S *mattress. The others follow him with their eyes. He steps softly over to* SMITTY *and cuts the ropes about his arms and ankles with his sheath knife, and unties the handkerchief over the gag.* SMITTY *does not turn around but covers his face with his hands and leans his head against the wall. His shoulders continue to heave spasmodically but he makes no further sound.*]

DRISCOLL—[*Stalks back to the others—there is a moment of silence, in which each man is in agony with the hopelessness of finding a word he can say — then* DRISCOLL *explodes:*] God stiffen us, are we never goin' to turn in fur a wink av sleep? [*They all start as if awakening from a bad dream and gratefully crawl into their bunks, shoes and all, turning their faces to the wall, and pulling their blankets up over their shoulders.* SCOTTY *tiptoes past* SMITTY *out into the darkness . . .* DRISCOLL *turns down the light and crawls into his bunk as*

[*The Curtain Falls*]